bang the
keys

four steps to a lifelong writing practice

by Jill Dearman

ALPHA   A member of Penguin Group (USA) Inc.

ALPHA BOOKS

Published by the Penguin Group

Penguin Group (USA) Inc., 375 Hudson Street, New York, New York 10014, USA

Penguin Group (Canada), 90 Eglinton Avenue East, Suite 700, Toronto, Ontario M4P 2Y3, Canada (a division of Pearson Penguin Canada Inc.)

Penguin Books Ltd., 80 Strand, London WC2R 0RL, England

Penguin Ireland, 25 St. Stephen's Green, Dublin 2, Ireland (a division of Penguin Books Ltd.)

Penguin Group (Australia), 250 Camberwell Road, Camberwell, Victoria 3124, Australia (a division of Pearson Australia Group Pty. Ltd.)

Penguin Books India Pvt. Ltd., 11 Community Centre, Panchsheel Park, New Delhi—110 017, India

Penguin Group (NZ), 67 Apollo Drive, Rosedale, North Shore, Auckland 1311, New Zealand (a division of Pearson New Zealand Ltd.)

Penguin Books (South Africa) (Pty.) Ltd., 24 Sturdee Avenue, Rosebank, Johannesburg 2196, South Africa

Penguin Books Ltd., Registered Offices: 80 Strand, London WC2R 0RL, England

International Standard Book Number: 978-1-59257-914-3
Library of Congress Catalog Card Number: 2009920705

11   10   09   8   7   6   5   4   3   2   1

Interpretation of the printing code: The rightmost number of the first series of numbers is the year of the book's printing; the rightmost number of the second series of numbers is the number of the book's printing. For example, a printing code of 09-1 shows that the first printing occurred in 2009.

Printed in the United States of America

For my parents, Audrey and Hal, for every encouraging word, for every book, from Marjorie Morningstar to Compulsion, with all my gratitude.

Contents

Step 4: Go 179

Appendixes

Foreword

"Hell, man, I know very well you didn't come to me only to want to become a writer, and after all what do I really know about it except you've got to stick to it with the energy of a benny addict." So says Sal Paradise, the narrator of Jack Kerouac's *On the Road*, in response to the most shameless of cons: teach me how to write. Sal's advice seems to me about right. Becoming a writer means, among other things, organizing your life around a compulsion: acting selfishly; alienating or imposing upon friends; boring strangers; stealing from acquaintances; deluding yourself; abusing your financial health; returning compulsively to dark alleys; and prostrating yourself before people who don't care.

The people who love you wish you would quit already. But still we keep at it, like our friend the Benzedrine freak, because some beast inside us feels unfed if we do not. As Jill Dearman notes, the act of inventing people and actions is as close as we come to the divine act of creation. Unlike the benny addict, who wants only to consume, writers want to procreate. Writing is—or at least ought to be—a natural part of being human. We encounter the world through characters and images, and make sense of it through stories. We are story-making creatures. And yet the biggest obstacle is often simply getting started, or getting up once we have been knocked down, as inevitably we will be.

There are plenty of books about how to write, just as there are about how to lose weight, and I suspect the batting average for both is about the same, somewhere around zero (though a diet book espousing benny addiction might kill two birds). It's safe to assume that William Faulkner didn't write *Absolom, Absolom!* by reading a really good chapter on how to "Tighten Up Your Metaphors." And neither will you.

But let us learn something from the benny addict. Addicts don't say, "Maybe I'll take care of my jones next week." Instead, they will do anything to eliminate the obstacles that keep them from the thing they want.

Bang the Keys is about purging those internal obstacles that prevent us from getting our stories out, or that clip them along the way. Writing can look like magic to everyone but the writer: to her it looks like the courage to sit in front of a blank screen and the discipline to stay there. The most dashing writers, even Kerouac, can be identified not just by their genius, but by their work ethic—the doggedness with which, even when the blank page looks like a tombstone, they sit down and bang the keys.

The ancient Greeks believed that muses breathed epics into their poets, complete, and that all the poets had to do was open themselves to the muses, then deliver the goods fully and bravely. They didn't need to invent them; the stories were already there. So it is with our stories, however modest or epic. Everything we need to know about them is already banging around somewhere in our heads, consciously or not. The pages that follow offer strategies for reaching them, nurturing them, and facing the uncomfortable truths to which they lead us. The way isn't easy; you'll probably fall short most of the time. If it were easy, we'd all write like Alice Munro and have slender waistlines.

In *On the Road*, it takes Sal the entire book to learn how to tell his story, until finally, after a novel's worth of suffering and adventure, an old man approaches with the words, "Go moan for man." Jill Dearman offers this advice: "Choose Art Over Idiocy." Like Kerouac's, it's the harder road, especially now, when idiocy is so juicy and accessible. But writing is both human and divine, and in the end, it is … dare I say it … maybe … under the right circumstances … possible.

—John Leland, New York City, November, 2008
Staff reporter, *The New York Times* and author of the books *Why Kerouac Matters: Lessons from 'On the Road'* and *Hip: A History*.

Introduction

November 2003. On a chilly Wednesday night, I ventured up-town with my sister Penny to a Torah class led by Rabbi Simon Jacobson. On that evening, in a musty, medium-sized classroom, he read a portion of the Torah and likened the ancient tale to a modern concept: the mission statement. Every business has one; without it the goals of the company would be muddled, unclear. A mission statement provides focus, and should be written in concise, precise language. It should be short and clear enough, the rabbi explained, that if a company executive ran into an old colleague on an elevator, he could express the concept quickly enough for the colleague to hear it before he exited the lift. So he challenged us, why don't each of you write a mission statement for your life?

Brilliant! I'd never heard this idea before (though I have heard it many times, in many different realms, since—clearly it's a concept with legs!). Immediately, I attached to it. The rabbi continued his lecture, but I could barely contain my excitement. The moment I got home, I planned to write my mission statement.

Two hours later:

The *Law and Order* episode that night was a good one. A middle-aged couple took their dog for a morning walk through Central Park when the old mutt stumbled upon a dead body ....

About a year later:

I was riding on a commuter train to New Jersey, for a health conference I was covering. It was early in the morning, and I was still waking up. Sipping on my coffee, I rummaged through my knapsack for a book, a Walkman, a notebook. Overwhelmed by choice, I closed my eyes, hoping sleep would clear my head. It was the week of my birthday and as I drifted into a doze, a memory jolted me to full consciousness. The mission statement for my life. Uh, yes, that one. I had not thought of it, but for a passing moment here and there, since the Torah lecture the year before. But now, halfway between a headache and Wayne, New Jersey, I felt a strong compulsion to write it. No thinking. No excuses. This is what I wrote:

My mission is to support other writers in their attempts to master their work, while continuing to develop my own craftsmanship as a writer. I will do all this in service and homage to written language, in all its varied forms.

I was shocked by how much these words resonated with me. They felt right. What surprised me was what I led with: other writers. What about me?! I had been teaching for the past three years at the New York University School of Journalism, and my writing workshops, which I'd started almost two years earlier, were gaining popularity. Executive Directrix and glamour-gal Donna Brodie, along with "El Staff" at the Writers Room (an urban writer's colony in New York City), helped spread the word.

That fall I had added extra sections, until I was teaching workshops back to back. Many highly respected magazine editors, TV writers, and screenwriters joined the fun. I had just begun curating the Writers Room Reading Series at Cornelia Street Café. It was a truly raucous and energized time, and it all revolved around supporting other writers, while I developed my own writing, while paying homage to the written word—through reading, study, and the sharing of books. And it certainly seemed as if everything I taught my clients and students only helped me with my own work, just as every heartbreak and success, every moment of insecurity or sudden burst of confidence, were all parts of the writer's life that I could empathize with.

I had found a calling.

Yet until I put it down on paper, on that New Jersey Transit train, I could not see it so clearly. Before teaching the workshops, coaching private clients, and formally teaching at NYU, my sole focus as a writer was me. Me! Glorious me! I had a diligent practice; I'd had bolts of luck and recognition in the book publishing world and in the journalism world, but I couldn't escape an inner voice that sounded like a persistent (and quite irritating!) whine. The whine of my writerly ego demanding more attention.

As my focus grew less self-directed, that whine shifted from a high-pitched, birdlike "caw" to a low-I've-left-the-stereo-on-but-nothing's-playing kind of buzz. I was moving in the right direction! Still, it was a process, making the shift from caring only about me, as a writer, to caring deeply about the work, and writing lives, of other scribes. It took still more time to find a balance. As anyone who teaches writing knows, it's easy to get so involved in the instruction and mentoring of others that your own work gets less attention.

In so many ways, that mission statement was a true foreshadowing. The more I wanted to support other writers, the more (it become clear) I had to support my own writing. The Dalai Lama, in all his Holiness (and, people, let's admit it, all his adorableness!) says that you must first feel compassion for yourself and then let it spread out. I stopped judging my inner whine-o, and did a bit of Jungian engaging with my Shadow. Needy ego assuaged, I was able to look outward, at what I had to share with other people.

Somehow this Buddhist instruction regarding compassion was a perfect complement to the wisdom I happened upon from a rabbi. In Kabbalist teaching, the idea that humans, just like all other animals, are wired with the desire to receive is a given. There is no point denying this primary part of our nature. And if any of you have ever taken a road trip with a Jewish family, you know it's true. One mile out of the city, and suddenly everyone is a certified hypoglycemic who needs constant sustenance! In Kabbalist thought, the idea is to receive ... for the purpose of sharing with others. So pack enough bagels for everybody. (Or whatever panic snack attack of choice your people enjoy!)

As writers that means we need to read other writers (darling, hello!), and basically receive the world of literature (and its comrades in film, theater, television, and art), and share what we learn about story, practice, and everything else that matters in a writer's life, with our fellow scribes.

Bang the Keys is really a Writing Workshop in a Book.

It is written for writers who work in any form, and at any level— from newbie, to working writer, from professional at the top of his game (and oh the pressure to bang out the next one), to a midlife writer, standing like Dante in the dark wood, weary from the past and unsure of where to go next.

If you are so inclined, e-mail the other writers you know (who are undoubtedly complaining they have no time to write!) and arrange to meet with them for a month: once a week, for four weeks, three hours per meeting (math whizzes, that's a total of twelve hours—assuming I correctly carried the one?). Each section in this four-part book deals with a separate step in developing your writing practice. As a writing coach, I am described as nurturing but whip-cracking and that's the tone of the tune, baby doll! My workshops are not critiquing workshops, so if you gather with your buds, wait till the workshop is over before (optionally) sharing work. The exercises, however, are fun and fruitful to read aloud with your group, if you so desire. The goal is to bang the keys—on your typewriter!

Bang the Keys is culled from six years of leading workshops and coaching clients, as well as many, many more years of writing and reading, pitching and publishing, getting rejected and revising, celebrating and commiserating with every type of writer you can imagine. I've received the rare privilege of serving as confidante to so many wonderful prose writers, screenwriters, playwrights, television writers, and graphic novelists, that I can honestly state: there is no medium or genre that feels foreign to me, and no writerly feeling or experience that I can't relate to. Yet continually, I've seen that it's the writers who live in service to the written word, share their wisdom with other writers, and read as much as they can who are the most fruitful, successful, and happiest writers of all. That's the writer I aspire to be, on a daily basis, and so far it's working beautifully, even on the most frustrating, stuck-in-my-own-rut/oppressed-by-the-man days! (Note to self: when in that mood, try playing the '70s song "Car Wash" for an endorphin rush.)

Besides, in our current interactive age, we are all ubiquitously connected anyway. E-mail and the Internet (with its temptation to "research" all the day long, instead of write) are two of the biggest obstacles almost all my clients, my fellow writers (and I) face every day—every minute, it seems!—in this Googly, modern world of ours. More distractions are in the hopper, I'm sure, as the speed of our world just keeps increasing.

Part of my inspiration for writing this book, and writing it now, is to communicate with writers of our era. The wisdom I've culled from leading the writer's life, and the exercises I've created by coaching writers of all stripes are (I hope) eternal. Some of the style and skills, however, are a direct and organic response to the multitasking, inescapably wireless world that we live in. Even if you think of yourself as slow-paced, fine and mellow, I can't imagine you live outside the influence of our century, with all its infomania and ongoing technological advances. (No disrespect to the Amish, of course!)

My mission for this book is to provide you with a nonformulaic formula for developing a millennial-world writing practice that you can integrate into your life, and use again and again, even as technology further evolves and more high-tech interruptions continue to intrude. Hell, even if we experience some actual version of Y2K, and lose all our virtual systems, our brains have become so universally A.D.D. that we would still need all the help we could get to keep our concentration focused—on our practice.

You can use this book as a course, to learn with writer friends as a group, or read it solo for help on your current writing project, and again on the next one, and on, and on, until the practical exercises and soulful steps are second nature. Ultimately, of course, you alone must do the work, but my aim is true, and it is truly to show you that you are not alone, little pencil-pusher, dear keyboard banger. And the more fortified you become as a writer, the more reliable and self-regenerating your writing practice becomes, the more I hope you will share your wisdom with other writers.

So riddle me this, dear readers: What is your mission?

(Be advised: you don't have to go to New Jersey to answer that question ... but if you do, please deliver a shout-out to Bruce.)

I invite you to share your responses to this book by e-mailing me at jill@jilldearman.com. I promise to post some of the most relevant and riotous replies on my blog at www.bangthekeys. com.

Now, read on and Bang the Keys!

—Jill Dearman, writer's friend
Brooklyn, New York, 2009

Acknowledgments

Thanks to D.B. and the Writers Room in New York City where my practice began to thrive, and to Steven Rosen and the Staff of A.G. for opening your wild doors to me. Thanks to Janet Rosen, my literary agent and angel in cashmere, and to my editor, Michele Wells, and the entire Penguin/Alpha crew, especially Dawn Werk, Ginny Munroe, Megan Douglass, Mike Sanders, Mike Dietsch, and Gardi Wilks. Thanks to my family for support, and my friends, especially Wendy Jo Cohen, who's shared all the writerly highs and lows. Special gratitude to the generous and multi-talented Joe Moran (www.joemoran.info) who designed my website (www.bangthekeys.com). Profound thanks to my clients for allowing me to be your confidante, your guide, and your playmate in the world of words; when we do what we do, we are at one with the gods of writing. Finally, thank you, Anne, my great love. You introduced me to the piano, and your very being is music in my life ... and to think, it all began for us at the Algonquin. How literary!

Trademarks

All terms mentioned in this book that are known to be or are suspected of being trademarks or service marks have been appropriately capitalized. Alpha Books and Penguin Group (USA) Inc. cannot attest to the accuracy of this information. Use of a term in this book should not be regarded as affecting the validity of any trademark or service mark.

1

acronyms and archetypes

"One chiefly needs swiftness in banging the keys."
—Mark Twain

"Punch the keys for God's sake!"
—Sean Connery, as a Salinger-esque reclusive writer, wildly hollers this line at a tentative young scribe in the Gus Van Sant film *Finding Forrester.*

All creations begin with a big bang like the grand one that began the universe, or the big bang from which each of us began (think about it … but not too hard). All writers know that our creations begin with an explosion of inspiration, but in order to harness that inspiration and develop it into a finished work of any kind, whether a short story, a memoir, or a play, we need to bang the keys frequently and fervently to bring the universe we imagine in our minds to life on the page.

But how can a writer follow through on his vision and bring his work to fruition in the world … and then hunker down and do it again on the next project? And again after that? In my work as a writing coach and university writing teacher, I have seen many scribes throw potentially good material in a drawer because they lacked the confidence and craft to complete it.

Yet I've also seen writer after writer build the foundation of a strong practice, based on eternal and true principles. I created my Bang the Keys system by adapting an inspiring bit of Talmudic wisdom and Native American belief into a practical but soulful system for writers.

The Bang Theory

In 2001, I was introduced to the concept of "Animal Medicine" within the Native American Way (see Chapter 10 and the appendix for more). In this tradition, the Butterfly represents transformation, which takes place in four stages:

1. The egg stage of an idea or thought.

2. The larva stage of choice.

3. The cocoon stage of realizing the dream.

4. The birth stage of sharing the completed idea.

In 2003, I attended a Torah lecture in which the creative process (according to ancient Jewish mystics) was likened to the process God used to create the universe. I have adapted what was first communicated to me in an esoteric way, into an accessible method, using four easy to remember steps that form the acronym, B.A.N.G.

The progression of steps in the creation of the universe, the rabbi (Rabbi Simon Jacobson, who was passing on wisdom from his

Rebbe before him) said, was very much like steps in the creative process. Each step was aligned with a letter in the Hebrew alphabet: Yud, Hei, Vav, Hei. Each letter, he explained, contains deep primordial meaning.

Yud, the spark that began the universe, is now the *B* for *begin*, for the only way to begin is simply to begin; Hei, the form the world takes, is now *A* for the *arrangement* of your ideas into a concrete shape (whether novel or nonfiction book, screenplay or sitcom script); Vav, which means "hook," as in the emotional hook or connection, is now *N* for the *nurturance* needed to nourish the creation, because if you don't love your work who will? And the final Hei is now *G* for *go*, the final letting go that will allow the work to live on in the real world.

To put it another way:

1. **Begin** with your strongest idea.

2. **Arrange** your work into a concrete shape.

3. **Nurture** your project with love so that others may love it, too.

4. **Go.** Finish and let it go so it may live independently in the world.

These concepts will be further explained throughout the book.

Certain steps seem to come more naturally for certain writers, and the opposite is true, too. I've seen members of my workshop who are strong in the beginning (Step 1) but find it hard to really love their work (Step 3). Others may be great at creating an elegant structure for their project (Step 2) but may be so obsessed with perfection that they can't stop tinkering (Step 4). Still others can begin and end but can't seem to structure and nurture.

And a writer's strengths and challenges can change from project to project. Yet this structure has an eternal resonance. Begin. Arrange. Nurture. Go. And in order to fulfill the promise of these steps, all you have to do is sit there and bang the keys of your typewriter (or some other writerly device). Bang. Oh, do I love a good acronym!

Engaging with these four steps, for every draft, every project, again and again, is a way to engage with the world of your writing. But those fingers that do the bangin' are connected to the rest of you. Let's skip the anatomy review and cut right to the problem area: the mind. In lieu of a brain-ectomy, a writer is left with one good option, in her battle to bust a move, and put her words onto the page before depression or the drink destroy her nerve.

That option is to understand her own nature, engage with herself, so that she can then engage with her work.

What Kind of Writer Are You?

When I first became a writing coach, I was determined to be a model writer myself. I was rigid in my daily writing routine (not to mention my biweekly jazzercise routine), and I never missed a deadline. I was a diligent writer, but also a dictatorial one.

Then one day I brought in Brooke Berman, an award-winning playwright friend and colleague, as a guest speaker in my writing class at New York University. One student asked Brooke what she does when she is working on a play and the material is not coming. Does she push through regardless? Knowing how dedicated Brooke was, I expected her to say, "Absolutely!" Instead she replied immediately: "No. I don't push through! I work on something else. I trust that what I need will appear later."

That weekend I put aside the serious essay I'd been struggling over and allowed myself to write a wild short story. I went back to the essay soon after, and within months both pieces were accepted at prestigious literary magazines. Now I guess you could say I'm a reformed Dictator.

In my six years as a writing coach, with clients who are new to the word game, as well as top-tier writers and editors, I've noticed that almost all of my clients fall into four distinct categories. In addition to the Dictator, there are the Distractionist, the Perfectionist, and the Commitment-phobe. I describe them to help you identify which kind of writer you are. I also blend in some insights from Charles ("Chuck") B. Strozier, a therapist and Pulitzer Prize–nominated author of *Heinz Kohut: The Making of a Psychoanalyst*, and thoughts from Panio Gianopoulos, widely published essayist and short story writer, who also worked for many years as a book editor at Bloomsbury. "As an editor, I am definitely familiar with all four of those types," Panio told me. Chuck provides us with the Psycho-Analysis, Panio with the Editor's P.O.V.

If you recognize yourself in one of these profiles, don't throw in the towel yet! (Or if you're a Perfectionist, at least fold it neatly.) For every self-sabotaging habit, I offer some constructive solutions. By using the strengths of other types of writers, you can discover practical ways to break frustrating work patterns.

The Distractionist

This quick-thinking fellow is never at a loss for great ideas, but somehow loses interest by the second draft … or sometimes the second paragraph.

The Psych Evaluation

He is the story. The story is his being, and thus highly invested. To have it read and admired touches his grandiosity. But to have it denigrated is to experience a profound loss of self.

Editor's Take

I don't see the Distractionist much, but I have a couple of writer friends like that. They jump from project to project and format to format. It'll start out as the first chapter of a novel, then he'll rewrite it as a play, a few months later decide no no, it'll work as a memoir, eventually give up on that and switch to poetry … and a few months later, he's back to writing it as a novel. Personally, I think this is primarily a stalling technique, and has more to do with self-confidence (or a lack thereof) than a spirited investigation of formal possibility. (Perhaps this is actually the Commitment-phobe? Your call.) The best trick I can suggest is to tell the story in the *first* format that occurred to you. That's probably the right one. If, after you *finished* a first draft, it seems wrong, then try something else. The same principle applies to dating. Pick the one that made you excited and go with that one ….

Tips

The distractionist can learn from the Dictator (see below) by imposing strict deadlines upon himself. Journalist after journalist has come through my classes and all reported the same thing: deadlines force them to finish their articles, and they seem to be of great use when doing one's own work as well. Writing retreats are also a great help for Distractionists. If you can get into a colony, go, go! If you can take off a weekend or a week and rent a cabin in the country, go, go! If you have the money, or you are willing to disguise yourself as a bellhop, do what legendary poet Maya Angelou does: check into a hotel room to bang out your draft.

The Dictator

She knows how to keep her eye on the prize and her butt in the chair; yet her unwillingness to change her original vision as her discovery process evolves makes her inflexible and stiff— and often frustrated as the needs of readers and the marketplace evolve while she refuses to.

The Psych Evaluation

The Dictator is dealing with underlying anxiety and trauma. She can't afford to let go because any relaxation of the fortress of defense will bring the walls down. But the protective barriers make it difficult to tap into the full range of her creativity.

Editor's Take

Oh boy, have I worked with this one. They're refreshingly fo-cused writers, no question, but they can't compromise. They're usually fiction writers. The best recommendation? Go write an article for a magazine! Watch 80 percent of your work be changed. Then realize it's not the end of the world. Gain a little flexibility.

Tips

Because being too tightly wound is your problem, why not warm up by doing a little journaling, to release some anxiety before you begin your writing day? Practice the art of stretching by lit-erally stretching. A little yoga could put you in a more relaxed physical state, allowing you to get in touch with a looser writ-ing style. Take a page from the Commitment-phobe's book and work on what gives you pleasure for a while. As I did, ask your-self "What do I want to write?" And finally, mix it up: write at different times of the day, in different places.

The Perfectionist

She had us at hello, or whatever her first fabulous sentence was. Yet she cannot move on to the next brilliant line because she is still agonizing over the punctuation in the first.

The Psych Evaluation

Obsessive-compulsive. The dishes on the rack must be exactly ordered, the shoes under the bed just so. The precise forms of her writing matter more than the content because their purpose is to ward off the intrusive thoughts, impulses, or images that so threaten the self.

Editor's Take

This one speaks to me, as you know. I am a terrible Perfectionist. Writing a first draft is a nightmare because for the time it takes— months, years—I live in terror of a bus running me over and someone actually reading the sloppy prose I haven't had a chance to revise yet. The funny thing, however, is no matter how much I revise the first draft while writing it (no matter how often I go back when I shouldn't), when I *do* finally start the second draft, I am stunned at how sloppy the first draft is anyway. Or expendable, because I discovered, at the end of the book, a fact that makes entire swaths of arduously articulated prose irrelevant.

All that agonizing is pre-emptive and a hindrance. The best time to be a Perfectionist is the second draft. That's when it's a tremendous asset, and you should glory in it. My suggestion— and it's hard for Perfectionists, but try it—is to set small, distinct deadlines (finish chapter six by the end of next week, for example) and stick to them no matter how painful. And to make a deal with yourself that *no one* gets to read it until you're done with the second draft. The first draft is for your eyes only.

Tips

I coach many high-end magazine and book editors. They make their living by perfecting other people's copy. No wonder it is so torturous for them to tolerate a misplaced comma or a slack phrase. These Perfectionists find it hard to move forward because they are always going back to improve their prose.

One option: take a page from the Distractionist's book and write as if you are avoiding work by sending e-mails. Write a thousand words quickly, and then send it to a writing coach or fellow writer who is also working on a project. Once you've pressed "send" you can't change that draft. Move forward and revise this section when your entire manuscript is done.

Cecil Castellucci, young adult novelist (*The Queen of Cool*) and graphic novelist (*The Plain Janes*) observes: "The best flowers are fertilized by crap. You have to write that crappy first draft sometimes and just let it be."

My client Judith Pinsker, multiple Emmy Award–winning *General Hospital* writer, agrees: "You just have to write badly and let things happen from there. If you're lucky it will begin to flow eventually, and you can either go back and lop off the beginning or fix it. If you're less lucky and it's not flowing you have to keep writing anyway. Working on soap scripts taught me this. It is a relentlessly demanding job because as a colleague of mine once said, 'In soap opera there is no third act. It just keeps going.' If you expect to keep your job you had better turn in your work on time. There's nothing like fear of losing your contract to break a writer's block."

The Commitment-Phobe

It takes him a while to settle on one project. When he does, he becomes inexplicably obsessed with "the one that got away."

The Psych Evaluation

A hybrid. What lies beneath his ambiguous relationship to writing could be any or all of what is true of the other three. What is generally going on is an unproductive self-involvement. As with people, he flits from one story to another.

Editor's Take

I'm not sure how different this one is from the Distractionist, so I'll just mention a subcategory, which I'll call the Procrastinator. (Although all writers, in my experience, are procrastinators to some extent.) For this kind of writer, everything has to be just right or else the session is off. Hungry? Can't write. Only able to squirrel away one hour? Can't write. Sleepy? Antsy? Cranky? As I said, all writers struggle with this to some degree, but when it becomes particularly inhibiting for someone, I think it's important that he recast writing as a pleasure. It's a little luxury. Like getting an ice cream sundae. The conditions don't need to be perfect, because writing is the thing that makes all the other conditions of your life bearable. It sweetens.

Tips

Author Castellucci also understands the Commitment-phobe. "No one gets to read the book if you don't finish it," she says. "This happens to me all the time. I tell myself that if I finish what I already started, as a special treat I'll get to work on that new delicious idea. It's my reward for doing my work."

The Commitment-phobe can learn something from the Perfectionist's focus: use an egg timer to force yourself to work on one project for an hour. The more you get to know your project, the more likely you will fall in love with it and want to say "I do" … or even better: get to the final page and say "The End."

(Portions of the chapter were originally published in *The Writer* magazine, November 2007.)

Just as many sitcoms contain one episode in which the characters give up their bad habits by trading them with a buddy, you, too, can move past your played-out patterns by making good use of other writers' vices. For one week, why not put on a different type face? For example, if you are a Dictator, force yourself to spend an extra week perfecting (a la the Perfectionist) a page, rather than meeting your strict deadline of finishing your chapter in a month.

Please note, each chapter will include a series of related exercises; some focus on craft, some are meant to inspire, some are for problem-solving. Try doing them as you read, or else at the beginning of your writing sessions. Rather than face a blank page, warm up with a little exercise. Eighties legwarmers are optional.

Exercise: Pre-Meditation

Throughout the book you will be provided with dozens of writing exercises. Before you begin maniacally signing up for them like Marcia Brady on the first day of high school, allow me to provide you with some basic guidelines that will apply (unless otherwise indicated) to all the games we will play:

1. Light a candle: White for purity and clarity, unscented for the allergic in the room.

2. Take a minute or two to clear your mind with a mini-meditation. Try this: stare at the candle, and then close your eyes and try to "see" the flame (not the candle holder but the actual flame) in your mind's eye.

3. While you are picturing the flame, just breathe in and out, focusing on each individual inhale and exhale.

4. When you are ready to begin, take the "free-writing" approach. Just write without thinking about it. Keep your pen moving on the paper. Even if you don't know what to write, simply bang out the words, "I don't know what to write." More original, lively, and true words will come; I promise.

5. Take five minutes for each individual exercise, unless other- wise noted.

Note: *If you are working in a group, begin and end together. In between: no chit chat, please. Just chop chop! A group facilitator can call time at the beginning and the end. When five minutes are almost up, that person should quietly tell the group, "You may want to start to wind down now." When time is up just say, "Bring your final thought or sentence to a close now."*

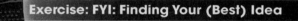

Exercise: FYI: Finding Your (Best) Idea

The only way to begin is to begin, my dears, so get out your pencil or pen, computer or typewriter, and get ready to search for and find your best idea.

1. "The Unusual Suspects."

Play good cop/bad cop and pretend your idea is a suspect you are interrogating. In dialogue form allow Good Cop, Bad Cop, and Suspect #1 to go at it. How would the Good Cop protect the Suspect? How would the Bad Cop verbally deci- mate the detainee? When time is up make a decision. Who has the better hunch about the Suspect, the Good Cop or the Bad Cop? If it's the former, consider this idea seriously. Do this exercise (five minutes at a time), for as many "suspects" as you wish. At the end, line up your suspects and pick your guy (or gal). Who's it going to be? Take your time, but be sure.

2."Intangible."

What is the intangible quality that draws you to this idea? To help put you in this mind-set, imagine you had to describe the "intangible" qualities of someone you truly love and desire. Spend a few minutes writing about this. Then spend the last couple of minutes writing about how you could bring the delicious, intangible qualities of this idea to life on the page … in an attempt to make the intangible tangible. This exercise is a little trippy, but give it a try. The only thing you have to lose is your mind!

3."Anonymous."

If your name were not on this project, would you still do it? Hash out this question on the page for five minutes.

4."Interview Yourself."

Are you the best person to write this story? Why? Why now? Think about it like this: Maybe you have three ideas. A screenplay set in Vietnam. A short story about an unconventional marriage. A memoir about your life as a vegan. There are a lot of people who are fascinated by Vietnam. A lot of people who have pondered the rules of marriage. A lot of vegans. Be a tough but fair interviewer so that you (as the interviewer) can determine which piece you (the interviewee) are best suited for and most ready to write.

5."Writing as Decision-Making."

After doing exercises one through five, now ask yourself: which is your best idea? Writing is all about making decisions, just like any job, just like raising a child, just like driving a car. Always so many decisions to make. You want to bring home a paycheck, right? You want to be a good parent, yes? You want to make good time on the road and arrive at your destination safely, don't you? Well, be just as adult and responsible with your writing. Just like decisions you have to make at work, at home, and out on the road of life, you can always make adjustments later, show flexibility, and live with doubt, but you must make decisions. Now which is your best idea—for you to write, right now, at this time? Write down the answer to that question ("I don't know" is unacceptable), in one sentence … now.

6. "Spark."

Now spend five minutes writing down everything you remember about when the spark of your best idea came to you, what was going on then? Free associate with abandon. For example, if you first had the idea in the shower at a hotel in Cleveland at your cousin's wedding, write down all you remember about the event, the people there, anything that you naturally connect to the particular time and place in your life when this spark of an idea first emerged.

Kudos, Kiddo(s)!

You began!

You took a baby step, and that was no small thing, baby. And if I may quote Bruce Springsteen and Dave Edmunds: "From Small Things, Mama, Big Things One Day Come."

Download the tune now, and dance around to celebrate. Then send me the YouTube video of your performance by going to www.bangthekeys.com. I will decide who has the best moves. Bruce and Dave, I invite you to be my co-judges.

2

the calendar effect

Congratulations. Now that you know what you are going to write, you are ready to tackle the next challenge: when are you going to write it? "Over the next month or two," is not a real answer, sweetie; it's an insult! If what you are writing means something to you, take it seriously. If the casual approach works for you, fine. Just sift through this book for the exercises and do your laidback thing, dude. For the rest of you, it's time to pull out your calendar. Any kind will do: a Google document, a Blackberry, a datebook, or that thing that's hanging on your wall filled with pictures of cute animals or hot cars.

Now open it up and put yourself on alert.

In Roman Polanski's classic horror film *Rosemary's Baby*, John Cassavetes circles two dates on the calendar and tells Mia Farrow, his anxious-to-conceive bride, that he's been a real beast as of late and he promises to make it up to her ... by impregnating her on one of those nights. The point, dear writer, is to set a date.

The late Donald M. Murray, Pulitzer prize–winning *Boston Globe* journalist, gave many talks on the theme "writing to deadline." He said that he'd been told that the word "deadline" originated from an actual line drawn inside a prison's walls. When the prisoners crossed that line they were shot down dead. He honored deadlines as a great impetus to write. If he did not meet them he imagined himself, like a prisoner, facing a firing squad, facing professional death.

Yet there is much within a deadline to make us feel alive, young, free. The pressure is on, so we've got to perform. It never gets any easier to face a deadline, and to face a blank (or messy, convoluted) page, but it's always stimulating and likely to produce great surges of creativity. Murray died at age 82 and his obituary included one of his ruminations on the writing process:

"Each time I sit down to write I don't know if I can do it. The flow of writing is always a surprise and a challenge. Click the computer on and I am 17 again, wanting to write and not knowing if I can."

Whether you are a cocky kid just starting out, or a Pulitzer prize–winning pro in your golden years, or somewhere in between, it never gets any easier. And that's the beauty of it. Remember: if writing were predictable it wouldn't be much fun. But keep this in mind, too, gentle scribe: if you don't sit down to do it, it won't get done!

In my writing workshops, I have found that six weeks is just enough time, but not too much, for most writers to handle. Clearly a major work cannot be completed in that time. But a short piece can, and a section of a larger work can, too. I tend to veer toward being cautious rather than ambitious when it comes to length. So don't be a size queen. Rather than aim for six essays in six weeks, how about two? Instead of a whole draft of your screenplay, how about act one? Lord knows if you meet your deadline and have time to spare you should use that extra time to write more, but I'd rather set you up for success than failure (I'm just sweet that way).

Exercise: The Big Clock

1. Mark it! Mark down a deadline for your project. As mentioned, a six-week deadline is usually quite workable. But you decide. Just set the date. If you are working with a group, everyone should choose the same date.

2. Name it! Name your baby. You wouldn't live with your three-week old infant without naming the child, would you? "My story" or "My memoir" is not enough. Make it real by once again *making a decision*. You can always change it later, but for now, show your work in progress the respect of giving it a working title.

3. Announce it! Every child could do with some good godparents and so can every writing project.

   If you are working with a group, go around in a circle and allow each person a few minutes to share the name of his or her project, the likely form (one act play, essay, etc.), and the gist of what it's about. Each person should also share a quantifiable goal with the group, as in "one draft of a short story, probably 15 pages," or "two chapters of my novel, probably 20 pages." Each person in the group should note the name of the writer, the writer's concrete goal, name of the writer's project, and form of that project. This helps the group to form a connection to the member's work.

> If you are working solo, send a note to a few friends sharing your plans and asking for their support in helping you to meet your deadline.

4. Work it! Two weeks before your deadline, jot down a reminder on your calendar. You may have to pick up your pace at that point. Put a one-week reminder in your calendar seven days before your deadline. The clock is a great motivator. This is all in the same spirit as a stage manager telling the actors in a play, "Ten minutes to curtain."

> It's showtime, folks!

Don't Toss the Garbage

Scott, a student of mine from my very first workshop, shared a moniker for the writer's first version of a project that everyone immediately connected to: the vomit draft. A disgusting yet true image. Most writers write their first drafts by spewing onto the page, without looking backward, letting their unconscious do the work. Then they do their shaping, refining, and polishing in the revision process. Yes, some writers must make their work perfect before moving on, and if that's your way, fine, but then I would suggest setting a very small goal size-wise. Perhaps six polished pages, or an individual scene in your short story, if that's your way.

And as for terminology: for the sake of the Maggie Smith–clutching-my-pearls part of me, let's clean up the phrase a little and call it a "garbage draft." After all, Stephen King famously threw his early draft of *Carrie* in the garbage; mercifully his wife Tabitha pulled it out and a career was born.

So do not literally throw those early drafts in the garbage! You'll find a way to use parts of this blessed mess to structure and polish something wonderful and complete. We'll get into structure quite deeply later on, but some of you may already be set on coming up with an outline before doing any work. The effectiveness of this approach depends on your nature, and the type of work you are doing. For traditional screenplays and television scripts, which rely much more on a set formula, you may want to outline. For fiction or creative nonfiction you may want to follow your imagination.

Flannery O'Connor wrote sentence by sentence, not knowing exactly where she was going. She famously recounted being surprised when a Bible salesman simply showed up on the page while she was writing her story "Good Country People." It was only after writing a draft that she would access the narrative threads she would then weave through the piece. But only by spitting out that draft, and struggling through its initial ugliness, could she leave us with eternally enduring tales.

Accountability

Whatever your writing method is, one thing is for sure: some element of accountability will help to ensure that you meet your goal. We get into writing buddies/sponsors in Chapter 3, but something you can do even before connecting with a buddy is to tell people your plan. That way instead of having bored slacker colleagues nag you to go to lunch, your real pals will nag you with e-mails asking "Did you finish your chapter yet?"

Another thing that works as real motivation is making a deal with yourself, and asking a friend to hold you accountable for following through on the contract. Stanley, a dedicated Democrat, promised to write a check for $100 to the Republican National Committee if he didn't finish a revision of his play by Halloween! No trick; no treat, right? He just had to do the work. His trick helped him reach his goal. Finally, let's go back to first principles, simplicity.

Pick a date and mark it on your calendar in blood ... well, if you're not the Satanic-ritual type, a red magic marker will do.

Form a Writing Habit

Now that the deal is sealed, let's get into the steps that will help you meet your commitment: your writing hours.

I'm talking about the time that you carve out to actually write. The writing hours. The building block upon which everything else depends. I am a big believer in starting small and building up your writing practice incrementally. As an astrologer, I liken this approach to how one should work with the planet Saturn. This particular planet has a harsh reputation. Even folks who know nothing about astrology may have heard of "the Saturn Return." This transit comes once every 29 years. The first one is usually the most significant. That is when all the many varied lovely fabulous options of life start to dry up. After spending your 20s with all doors open, in terms of relationships, career, money, etc., you then face 30, and see that if you don't start to make some choices, the universe may only offer you cast-offs and leftovers, if that.

Saturn is all about how we budget our time and how we bring our goals and dreams to fruition in the real world. Whatever it is you want to do: from learning Italian, to paying off debt, to writing your novel, Saturn can be a very helpful (if crotchety) old chum of a friend. How to work with this wise curmudgeon? Common sense! First, make a decision, and hopefully share your decision with your inner circle, who will then nag you about your progress. Next, set aside the time to make your goal a reality. If your aim is to play guitar and you only practice an hour a week, that's how good (or lame) you will be. The more time you put in, the more you front-load the hard work and commitment, the sooner you will become Jimi Hendrix. And don't panic yet: you won't die at age 27, choking on your own vomit, I can almost promise you that. Although if you read over your own rambling first draft too soon you may want to hurl!

The late, great Italian fabulist writer and fabulous thinker, Italo Calvino (*If on a Winter's Night a Traveler, Invisible Cities*) heavily referenced Saturn in an essay on writing called "Quickness." He understood that although Mercury symbolizes the swift thoughts that run through the brain, it is Saturn, the concentrated, dedicated craftsman, who brings those inspired thoughts into a permanent form.

Just remember this, excited scribes: consistency works much better over the long haul, rather than working at a fever pitch, merely to prove that you can. Approaching your writing in a manic way is a lot like going to the gym for the first time and picking up a 400-pound barbell. You may be able to do it. And the victory, for one second, will be sweet … until you are in the hospital moaning and groaning and swearing to never work out again. So before you end up in traction, eating Bon Bons (is that physically possible? someone fact check, please), I need you to commit to a series of writing hours.

Flannery O'Connor wrote this in a letter to a young writer friend, back in 1957:

> "I'm a full-time believer in writing habits, pedestrian as it all may sound. You may be able to do without them, but most of us only have talent and this is something

that simply has to be assisted all the time by physical and mental habits or it dries up and blows away." (From *The Habit of Being*, letters from Flannery O'Connor.)

O'Connor, who died at age 39, fought lupus and other physical problems throughout her life, so she literally did not have the energy to write for more than two hours at a time. But that schedule worked out pretty well for her, wouldn't you agree? In this same letter she goes on to advise her young writer friend to approach her writing hours when her mind and body are fresh, and not, for instance, after a day of teaching.

You need to choose times that will be the most productive for you. Figuring out those times is a process, but you have to start somewhere. You can always adjust your hours later.

Exercise: Writing Hours

1. Choose either two three-hour blocks or three two-hour blocks that you will commit to as your Writing Hours over the next six weeks. During those hours you cannot answer the phone, go online, do the dishes, or do time-filling *research*.

2. Specify where you will do your hours and with what tool. Example: in the library, on your laptop. (Sounds like the board game Clue, doesn't it? Fine. The fact is you can do it on your fire escape with your Aunt Shirley's Peach Frost lipstick just so long as you do it!)

3. Write down your hours in your notebook and on your calendar.

Keep in mind: flexibility is fine. If you have to skip your Tuesday from 8 to 10 P.M. slot one evening, because of theater tickets bought months ago, or some other excuse (yeah,

yeah … I know, I know), that's all right. Just make sure you
make up those hours to yourself before week's end. Too much
wiggle-room demeans the schedule, and gets the boss lady's
Irish up. Don't make me violent.

And I guarantee you, once you make this commitment all sorts
of strange and confusing distractions will line up to get in the
way of you and your writing hours. A few months before starting my first writing workshop, I read a profile in *The New York
Times* of surrealist painter and writer Leonora Carrington.
Elaine Mayers Salkaln, the journalist who journeyed to Mexico
to interview the great artist, then 85, encountered many mischievous misfortunes on this assignment and noted: "The
Hasidim believe that when you are embarking on a spiritual
quest, which in a way I am, the forces of impurity do their best
to interfere."

When I was about to begin an advanced version of my writing
workshop, I bought a painting from an abstract expressionist
painter whose work I passionately connected to. The artist
Iris Lezak (the former partner of poet Jackson Mac Low)
impressed me with her work, and with her working habits. This
tiny, dynamic woman, who was pushing 80, got up at 5 A.M. to
paint—for decades—and still follows this stoic routine.

I asked her if she had any helpful thoughts for my workshop par-
ticipants in regards to developing an artistic practice. I wanted
to know: How does she stay so disciplined? How does she "show
up" for her practice even when she's not in the mood?

This was her reply: "Consciousness is work, so I'm always working. Even when I'm sleeping my unconscious is working to give

me dreams that illuminate my awake time. I'm always either coming down from finishing a painting or preparing to start again. Even when I'm not actually doing something, there seems to be a constant undercurrent of speculation about what to do next. Discipline and mood are not words that enter into my thinking about my process. Desperation does, and that has often been some physiological and psychological impasse that I can clear up only by painting. Take the pain out of painting and I'd be out of a job. Recently, and this possibly has to do with the mellowing of age, I rarely have to work from that kind of motivation. Now it's more restlessness: nothing is happening, and nothing is going to happen unless I make it happen, so I do."

Soon after, I received complementary words of wisdom from my friend Chitra who works high up in marketing, in the publishing world. I told her that I was quitting a tired freelance writing gig I had held on to for too long. This gig was something I could do easily but which no longer had meaning in my life, and which took away from the writing and teaching that mattered most to me. Simply put: I was whoring myself out! My wise old friend validated my decision to quit, and told me that in her profession they had an expression for this: *Focus on your core business and get rid of the distractions.*

Begin to take note of the distractions that exist in your life. When you can identify them, you can eventually extract yourself from their hold on you and then you can truly begin your project, and your writing practice.

Fear not; the issue of distraction will be dealt with in later chapters. It's an issue that never goes away, especially in the intrusive, hyperactive, yet strangely internal millennial world we live in.

Still, it is indeed the hours that you must come back to again and again and again. An athlete preparing for a game cannot rely upon the training he did the year before, or the month before for that matter. He needs to get into a routine and stick to it. If he misses a day because he is sick or has an emergency, or simply because he decided to rebel against the rigidity of his schedule, he knows that he must return—to the mat, the track, the ring, the field—and recommit to his training. He may end up winning his game, and becoming a *contenduh!* Or he may lose himself in distraction and destruction and end up with a one-way ticket to Palookaville. Or he may end up somewhere in between. The only way for him to know what he's capable of is to keep practicing.

My friend Andrea Kleine, who began her career as a performer/choreographer, has shifted her focus over the last several years into writing; she's won awards for her writing and maintains a highly disciplined practice. She has been known to say, "Dancers can only dance for so long; there's no age limit for a writer."

So just be glad you don't have to run in freezing cold winter snow or put on a tutu! Warm up your fingers and do your hours; bang those keys, you palooka!

Kudos, Kiddo(s)!

You set a deadline.

You named your project and decided upon a quantifiable writing goal.

You scheduled your writing hours.

You have built a foundation for a strong writing practice, thereby making this process real … mighty real!

3

sponsors (partners-in-crime)

I'm a dabbler. One super-chilled vodka martini or one warm, cozy cognac will do me just fine on occasion. And once in a while I can really throw 'em back, when need be! (To save our country or some such crisis.) But the old world equation of writer = active alcoholic is not so in vogue these days, is it? Richard Yates, Dorothy Parker, James Agee, Delmore Schwartz, we hardly knew ye. Yet even though this hazard of the business appears to be on the wane, 12 step programs abound. It is from Alcoholics Anonymous (AA), in fact, that I have adapted the "sponsor" system for writers. In AA, a member chooses a sponsor, who is available for support during those about-to-slip-off-the-wagon moments.

Finding Your Partner-in-Crime

In my Bang the Keys workshops, we randomly put together pairs of writers, so that they can both "sponsor" each other.

I recommend the "random" approach to the more democratic approach of allowing friends to pick each other. It's not *just* because I'm a tyrant. The fact is, friends have patterns of communication that may be hard to break. The element of surprise and the freshness of getting some new feedback from a new person can energize your writing. And if you "randomly" end up with a pal, so be it, it must have been meant to be.

Exercise: Brought to you by Our Sponsor

This exercise is for a Writing Group. Keep reading for ideas on how to find a sponsor if you are working alone.

1. Put two sets of matching numbers, written on scraps of paper, in a hat. (If you have eight group members, that's two "1"s, two "2"s, two "3"s, and two "4"s.)

2. Pass the hat around so that each member picks a number.

3. Count to three and then everyone do a reality-show style "reveal" to see who shares their number. Now you are all matched with a sponsor. (If there is an odd number of people, the person without a partner can be a "floater," and check in with a different pair every week. Or, as a group, come up with your own alternative to this mathematical dilemma.)

4. Take 5 to 10 minutes to "meet and greet" your sponsor. Exchange contact information and decide how and when you want to communicate. I recommend two quick phone calls or e-mail check-ins per week.

Sponsors take a few minutes aside to meet and greet, and to trade contact info. The plan is for each person to check in with his sponsor a couple of times a week, for just a brief chat, or e-mail exchange simply to ask "How's it going?" I like writers to arrange ahead of time how they will check in with each other. Personally, I hate the unplanned phone call. Often it interrupts my writing time, or my time alone or with my partner. Therefore, a phone check-in for me would be a source of dread, not support. So see if you and your sponsor can come to an agreement regarding how to check in—phone, e-mail, in person. Certainly I've seen lovely sponsor relationships develop, in which the pair end up meeting for writing hours together in cafés, and getting a lot done.

Your Sponsor Relationship

Remember, the point of this relationship is not to have a new buddy to kill time with—it's to be accountable to an outside person. Your sponsor's job is to offer sincere support to you. If you are having a hard time getting up at 7 A.M. instead of 7:45 A.M., to have that extra time to write in the morning, perhaps your sponsor can give you a wake-up call? It works well for both parties, as your sponsor is more likely to come through for you, the person counting on the call, than he might be for himself. This arrangement puts both people into a writerly and responsible mind-set. It also offsets some of the loneliness of the writer's life.

This relationship is great for brainstorming ideas. Even just a quick e-mail chat exchange like the one that follows could mean the difference between getting in all your hours and banging out some helpful draft pages, and sitting in front of the TV, eating chips, and feeling guilty.

Let's peek in on this IM chat between two sponsors. At last count, Cate Blanchett and Robert Downey Jr. were being considered for these roles.

LazyJane: How's it going?

Guacamole6: Don't ask.

LazyJane: Whassup?

Guacamole6: Was supposed to write after work, but ended up staying late at the office and not getting much done.

LazyJane: I feel you. My kid had a play date this afternoon and I could've written but I ended up alphabetizing my books instead, then doing it again Z to A. So how's the writing going in general?

Guacamole6: So-so. I have this really demented high school teacher character who I'm having a lot of fun with, but I have no idea what I'm writing or where it's going. It started out as a pretty serious short story, but now it may be turning into a funny horror story.

LazyJane: Maybe you should just keep going in that direction.

Guacamole6: You don't think that's a cop-out?

LazyJane: No, it sounds fun. Besides this is the garbage draft, so just see what comes out. You can clean it up later.

Guacamole6: Cool. Anyway, every time I try to write "serious" fiction, I start to doze off. How 'bout you? How goes it with your memoir?

LazyJane: A little schizo. Just like my family!

Guacamole6: Yeah?

LazyJane: I did my hours on Monday and I wrote this really incredible beginning. All these memories of childhood came back. I could smell the leaves on the cherry blossom tree outside our house. It was incredible. But it's three days later and I'm afraid to do my hours tonight.

Guacamole6: Why?

LazyJane: I think I may have peaked. I was already thinking about how I want to write this scene about a boating trip I took with my twin sister when we were 11, but it seems so trite to me now.

Guacamole6: Look, where I grew up in Hell's Kitchen we never even heard of cherry blossom trees—or boats! So just see what comes out. I can guarantee you it will sound fresh to me.

LazyJane: Can I send you what I've got so far?

Guacamole6: Why don't we wait till we're finished with these drafts. Remember you told me you stopped working on this book for two years after your cousin tore apart the section on your messed-up stepdad? Seems like where you come from they think they're living in Peyton Place!

LazyJane: You said it! But that's why I think a pair of fresh eyes would help me figure out what direction to go in.

Guacamole6: I promise, after you meet your goal—two chapters, right? I'll take a look and give you some general feedback. I just don't want to oppress you with my stupid suggestions. You've got a family for that.

LazyJane: Lol! Ok, do you want to check in again on Saturday?

Guacamole6: Sounds like a plan, man. And have fun writing tonight. I will be thinking about your boat trip.

LazyJane: Thanks. And have fun with psycho high school teacher.

Guacamole6: I will, assuming he doesn't chop me to bits! Bye.

LazyJane: Bye. Oh! By the way, what's the "Guacamole6" handle all about anyway?

AutoMessage: Guacamole6 is no longer online.

Give you a sense of how to play this game, dear reader? The key is a spirit of non-attachment, being present, and general good-will. If you are too invested in telling your buddy what to do, maybe you should tone it down. Another AA motto I love: keep your side of the street clean. Think about it.

You don't have to be a genius or a saint to be a good sponsor. Just offer an encouraging prod, listen, and don't fall into traps that a needy buddy might throw your way. Guacamole6 (and you'll have to kill me and every Bay Area drag queen on this planet to find out what that name means) was wise not to agree to read LazyJane's work while it was in progress. That's not what this program is about. I think every seasoned writer knows this. You have to muddle through, write pages you detest, pages you love, and everything in between, and somehow just keep going. A sponsor is really just there for a sense of camaraderie, to fight the loneliness of your new practice, and to offer a helpful word or two. Less is more.

The most important aspect of the sponsor relationship to remember is this: it must be equal. All writers are needy. Believe me, I'm checking my Amazon.com reviews right now! It seems as if Guacamole6 is a little bit more mature than LazyJane. But let's give LazyJane props for being just as willing to give to Guac as she was to receive. If you are a really great listener and you are paired with a really oblivious complainer, my heart goes out to you, buddy. That's why I ask each person to self-monitor and make a conscious effort to keep the relationship balanced, so that both parties get what they need. Use this Sponsor Oath as your guide.

Sponsor Oath

1. We agree to the method and time (e-mail, text, phone call, Monday and Friday mornings) by which we will contact each other for quick check-ins a couple of times a week.

2. We vow to focus on issues concerning our writing practice, not our porn habits, fashion crises, etc.

3. We aim to be constructive. If we are not sure how to be helpful, we will ask, "what do you need from me?" If we are not getting what we need, we will directly ask for it, not snipe behind each other's backs or seethe in silence.

4. We will table the urge to share work that's in process. (Exercises and tiny tastes of prose are fine, but no more.)

5. We will each strike a balance between talking and asking for support, and listening and giving support.

6. We will respond to each other's messages and not ignore them, but also not overwhelm the other person with a bazillion interruptions.

7. If the relationship is causing stress instead of relieving it and we can't seem to get what we need from each other through direct communication, we will seek help from a designated third party.

If you can contain yourself enough to not talk about graphic sex and violence in front of your little kids, or if you can be thoughtful enough to check in on a sick relative and ask how she's doing, and really listen for a few minutes, without then turning around and rambling about your day for 20 minutes, then you can train yourself to be a good sponsor.

When I'm leading workshops I always let folks know that they can come to me, confidentially, and say "My sponsor is a nightmare!!" And I will diplomatically intervene. (It happens all the time. People simply disappear. There's a swamp just outside the state line ....) That's why you may choose to elect a group leader, a person to smooth out any small problems in the group. More than "nightmare sponsors," though, what I've seen, sadly, is one sponsor simply opt out of the implied "contract," for no good reason. One person calls or e-mails in good faith, and gets no response. She tries again. Nothing. Karma, people. You don't want to come back in the next life as a slug do you? Then stop acting like one now, and do unto your sponsor as you'd like your sponsor to do unto you. Now!!

You Don't Need a Group or Writers Community to Find a Buddy

If you are working through this book solo, you can summon up a writer friend in your life to be your sponsor, and vice versa.

If that's truly impossible, just ask a good friend to do this for you, for a month. In return, you can offer to sponsor him in whatever way he wants—perhaps he's moved to the suburbs, drives everywhere now, and has put on a few pounds. Over the years he's been an on-again, off-again runner.

Why not check in with him about his running, his workout routine? Put on a sweat suit, wear a whistle, and be his coach; you may just love it. Again the philosophy is the same: you help him; he helps you.

Who knows, maybe you will start running, too, and he'll start writing, or just journaling.

Not a bad idea, actually ...

Your Writing Discipline Spills Over

There was a recent *New York Times* article about how developing discipline in one area helps with developing discipline in another area, and I've seen it in my own life and in the lives of friends, clients, countrymen ...

When I am in one of my most productive writing grooves, I get the most exercise and watch the least amount of television. I also take a page or two from Rocky's book and drink a glassful of raw eggs, punch a giant slab of raw meat, and run up the steps of the Philadelphia Art Museum as a cavalcade of energetic children cheer me on. I'm just literal that way, I guess.

The imagery may be a little too 1970s for today's times. (Who imbibes that much cholesterol and gets so intimate with non-organic beef anymore?) But the sentiment still holds.

Committing to a short-term, intensive writing goal is a lot like being in training. I work as a coach with my private clients, and play Personal Trainer of the Typewriter for them ("Bang those keys!!!"), but a good way to develop your writing muscles is to train with a fellow writer (or if not, any other fellow in training).

My friend Wendy Jo Cohen and I have been "writing buddies," or sponsors, for years. When we are screwing up our lives we throw this mantra at each other: "Choose art over idiocy!" That usually induces a return to the keyboard, and a stop to any destructive or depressive tailspins.

We first met years ago, in college, and as she noted, "We spent the first 10 years of our friendship destroying our bodies, and all the years since repairing them!" (How were we to know all those pitchers of beer and pounds of David's Cookies were bad for us? The science just wasn't *there* yet.)

Wendy and I had a good, long phase of going for a swim and sauna and then having a writing meeting, to catch each other up on our work.

Sponsors, training buddies, writing pals, partners-in-crime, or whatever you call them. Just make sure you *do* call them. Hopefully you will continually remind each other: choose art over idiocy!

Kudos, Kiddo(s)!

You found a sponsor and you committed to giving that person support, and receiving support as well.

In the Hebrew alphabet, the fifteenth letter, Samech, is connected to the concept of "support." This is no small thing. The world is interconnected, and we all lean on each other, in some way. When you have finished your work, most likely you will want to either get it out in the world professionally, which entails enlisting the support of agents, editors, marketing folks, etc., or you may just want to share it with friends and family. Either way, you will need other people. So in that spirit, big kudos to you for seeking out and giving support. Make this partnership work, to the best of your ability. Do it in support of your project, your baby; and as a sign of good faith to your godchild, your sponsor's baby.

And, baby, three chapters in, you have finished the preparation needed to begin working on your project. The foundation for your writing practice is set. Kudos!

step 1

begin

Begin with your strongest idea.

4

cahiers

"I never travel without my diary. One should always have something sensational to read on the train."—Oscar Wilde

"I tried to keep one, but I never could remember where I put the damn thing. I always say I'm going to keep one tomorrow."
—Dorothy Parker

Writers tend to be addicted to notebooks. It's a relatively inexpensive habit, but it's one that I challenge any pencil-pusher to kick. Actually, I'd never throw down that gauntlet, because I think it is a healthy and delicious habit—decadent yet (shall we say) *heart-smart*, like a bite of dark chocolate after every meal.

I enjoy reading writers' journals. From Franz Kafka's I learned that the man really *was* as tormented as we all assumed. From Sylvia Plath's diaries, that she was competitive and hungry for fame as a poet and author. From Joyce Carol Oates's: the reason

she is known as the most prolific writer of our time is because …
she is a consistent and disciplined writer, who constantly writes!

A couple of summers ago, my partner Anne and I went up to the
coast of Maine for a week in August. On our way, we stopped
in Portland and stayed over with our friends Alice and Ken. I
was looking through Alice's books in the guest room, and came
across *Heat*, a collection of Joyce Carol Oates stories.

Immediately immersed, I asked Alice if I could borrow it.
I remembered reading *Where Are You Going, Where Have
You Been?* as a teenager, then in my 20s reading her short,
Chappaquiddick-inspired novel, *Dark Water*. That weekend in
August, however, I packed Alice's book in my bag, took it up the
coast, and proceeded to read Ms. Oates's oeuvre of stories for
the rest of the next year. And what a joyous reading year it was.

The following August, Anne and I returned to the coast of Maine
again, and stopped in Portland on the way as we had the year
before. I returned the book to Alice and she said that she, too, had
gone through a hungry period of devouring Oates. It's easy to do!
The material is so rich, and it seems to be never ending.

That same year, *The Journal of Joyce Carol Oates 1973-1982* was
published, and I eagerly picked it up. I was shocked by what I
discovered: no drama. None. It seems that Ms. Oates wrote and
wrote, and suffered over her characters and plots, but it felt to
me like a good kind of suffering, a suffering which all committed writers live for.

The Buddha (if I may be so bold as to conjure the little darling
now) said that "all life is suffering." Where the Buddhist message becomes distorted is when people jump to the conclusion
that this thought is a downer. Of course we all see sickness and

death in our lives, we have to deal with change and loss which can be painful ... and it is natural, of course, to suffer during these times. The unnatural suffering comes when we attach other meanings to these realities. Because a dear loved one dies, perhaps someone who was one of our touchstones, we may say to ourselves, "No one will ever understand me again." The reality is, "I miss this person. I miss talking to her. I am sad that I will never experience that particular joy and sense of kinship, with her, again."

As writers, the kind of suffering that is natural could include the time it takes to discover the true nature of a work of art we are creating; the frustration over writing and writing and then having to throw away what we write when we realize we've gone down blind alleys; and the harsh reality of dealing with the business part of writing: pitching, promoting, rejections, criticism, etc.

Type Your Angst on the Page

All that is good suffering, because it means you are living the life of a writer. And if that is what you are, then that is good! Bad suffering is the unnecessary torment you put yourself through by *not* writing. To help you in the act of writing, a couple of special notebooks are a must. Patricia Highsmith often juggled two journals on a regular basis, throughout her life. Cahiers, she called them (French for notebooks). One cahier included notes on the book she was writing. Let's call this one a Project Cahier or "PC." The other was more of a diary and something she found useful for maintaining a "record of emotional experience" (according to her slim and tasty compendium: *Plotting and Writing Suspense Fiction*). I call it an Inner Cahier or "IC".

Highsmith was an intuitive writer who did her hours in bed with coffee and cigarettes. She often made notes in her PC right before going to sleep. Like many writers she understood that the unconscious mind has a knack for problem solving (see Part 3 for more, darlings!).

For our purposes, I always recommend summoning up your inner Uriah Heep and starting 'umble, as in one cahier. But when you are ready, move on to a second.

To get started, purchase two special notebooks or "cahiers," designating one a Project Cahier and the other an Inner Cahier.

Notes on Your Project

Your Project Cahier is the place to keep track of your thoughts and ideas on whatever writing project(s) you are working on.

Make a note in your Project Cahier every day. Notes could include content quandaries ("How am I going to weave in the back story of my villain's first marriage?") or random notes-to-self ("Write about the terrain of Dublin in as much detail as I can").

The best times to write in your Project Cahier tend to be right before bed or at the start of the day. Those are often a writer's freshest times. But any time will suffice. And write in it as much as you wish; carry it on your person at all times, including in the bath (purchase a zippered plastic contraption as necessary).

The point is to communicate with your Project Cahier as if it were a person, a person you were obsessed with (or if this works better for you, a Realtor who is scouting around for some dream property for you). In either scenario, no one would have to tell you to get in touch with your crush or your Realtor. You'd be looking for an excuse many times a day. And if you can get in the habit of writing in your Project Cahier every day, you will manage to stay obsessed with your project, I promise you.

Notes on Your Real Experiences, Observations

The Inner Cahier can be used every day as well, at your discretion, but is most useful in detailing what you feel when major highs and lows take place. The goal is to document your emotional experience within 24 hours of the actual incident. (Example: major fight with your boss. Get it down on paper that night or the next day. Include feelings, dialogue, observations of your physical environment as you sat in his office, as you seethed on the bus ride home, etc.) A couple of years from now you may be working on a screenplay that centers around a law firm. Perhaps you will use the physical details you noted in your cahier along with the visceral emotional experience, to make your script feel real, not contrived.

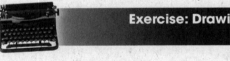

Exercise: Drawing from Your Inner Cahier

1. Write down a recent event that really got your blood up. Include as much real-life emotion and observed detail as you can manage.

2. Make a note in your calendar to revisit this Inner Cahier entry in exactly two weeks. Chances are, rereading this entry will immediately bring back the feelings you experienced.

3. Now like an actor practicing sense memory, write a three-page scene for your project, in which you weave parts of this entry into your story.

Ideally, we would aim to write daily, but that is not always possible. But what we can do is stay in touch with our writing and our writing selves. Alex Porter, a journalist who took my very first workshop (where we sat knee to knee in a fifth-floor walkup in Greenwich Village. How bo-ho, darlings!), said this to our group and it really resonated: "Writing is like fishing. You've got to keep your line in the water."

If your cahiers are blank, here's a nice way to begin to ink them up ...

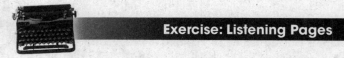

Exercise: Listening Pages

1. Read the nine quotes (that follow) from famous writers' journals, diaries, memoirs. Use any or all of these quotes as a "prompt," and write a page in response, in journal form (in your IC). Then in your PC, write a page of notes on how you can use this writer's thoughts as inspiration to make the content of your project that much richer.

2. Choose one of these writers to be your "listener." In your PC, write out some specific questions and concerns about the content of your work. For example, "What would help me to better illustrate the financial concerns of the towns-people in my story?" "What can I do to make my essay less sentimental and more humorous?" Write out this person's (imagined!) responses.

3. In your IC, write out a recent event that was filled with a lot of feeling for you. Ask one of the writers below to point out to you the small elements that stand out to him or her the most. Use the writer's "response" as a jumping off point to write another page, in which you go that much deeper.

Quotes:

A. "The first sentence was true. The second was invention. But to me—the writer—they had done something extraordinary."—V. S. Naipaul, "Prologue to an Autobiography"

B. "Is it true that if one once acquires a confidence in one's ability to write, nothing can miscarry, nothing is wholly lost, while at the same time only seldom will something rise up to a more than ordinary height?"—Franz Kafka, *Diaries,* May 29, 1914

C. "My money didn't last as long as I thought it would." —Paul Auster, *Hand to Mouth, a Chronicle of Early Failure*

D. "… the last producer I worked for spent about 15 minutes of time and about three or four inches of a personalized cigar, telling my agent that, vastly to his surprise, I was not a sole screenplay writer at all."—Raymond Chandler, *The Notebooks of Raymond Chandler*

E. "I was writing about up in Michigan and since it was a wild, cold, blowing day it was that sort of day in the story."—Ernest Hemingway, "A Good Café on the Place St.-Michel," *A Moveable Feast*

F. "The real return to normality is after falling out of love." —from a Patricia Highsmith notebook, mentioned at the end of Chapter 5 in *Beautiful Shadow: A Life of Patricia Highsmith* by Andrew Wilson

G. "Whenever you speak or write to me, remember that you do so to a man who neither can nor would dare to speak one word that is not the truth!"—August Strindberg, from *Letters of August Strindberg to Harriet Bose: Love Letters from a Tormented Genius,* edited and translated by Arvid Paulson

H. "But there is no point in writing a story about poor Bierstubbe, the TV writer who came to Rome to write a great play about sex; who was shortchanged everywhere, whose money flowed like water, who was depressed by the death of the Roman men and reminded of his own contested sexual identity, who wondered why he had ever left his cozy home, who drank too much gin at lunch, etc. So I will not write such a story."—John Cheever, *The Journals of John Cheever*

I. "Teaching is, in a way, the antithesis of art, which is permanent—or at any rate, as permanent as one might wish. The one falls away, the other remains. Yet both seem, to me, necessary: I would not want one without the other."—Joyce Carol Oates, *The Journal of Joyce Carol Oates 1973-1982*

Kudos, Kiddo(s)!

You have dedicated two notebooks to your work as a writer. Now you aren't just logging on to eight social networking sites and posting *about* what you are doing. You are actually *doing* something.

5

we can be heroes

Inevitably, in every workshop, and almost every private coaching session, writers suddenly realize they have chosen "the wrong project."

Perhaps you made a commitment, early in this little adventure of ours, to work on a short story you've been obsessed with for over a year. Then somehow, just when you've started to work on it with a real sense of purpose, a voice in your head says, "Forget it. I have to write a take-no-prisoners-to-hell-with-the-man-political-manifesto-essay-of-some-sort." (Yes, the voice in your head has a similar tone to that of a friend-with-benefits who might drunk-dial you at 2 A.M.)

This is a familiar quandary for most writers, especially in this era of multitasking and infomania! It seems that these days everyone is more plugged in and has access to more stimuli than ever. So perhaps the slow-food approach to writing fiction feels *too* slow for you. Thus the appeal of the manifesto or the wildly inspired novel you type out in one frenzied month.

Think you can bang eight Red Bulls and type out a tornado of righteous prose, single-spaced on a scroll, like Jack Kerouac on crack, right? Well, a little research into *On the Road* will reveal that Kerouac worked at his iconic book for years, and tried for six years after that to get a publisher, before it sold.

And sure, some writers can go back and forth between projects. Hermione Lee reports in her biography *Edith Wharton* that the famed fiction writer often juggled her work. She quotes Wharton during her chapter on *The Age of Innocence*, "I have never been able to write one novel without having another going at the same time, or at least two or three short stories, and I always return to my chief work stimulated by the change."

But perhaps it would be wise to get some solid work completed and then become a juggler on your next project(s)? So let's return to your current project.

Then again, maybe you are right. Maybe you made the wrong choice when you committed to working on your story. Or maybe you are having commitment anxiety, and suddenly you are like a just-married pig (and I mean that literally not figuratively), who suddenly realizes there are so many other babes to bang right after you bussed the bride!

How to know? How to know?

Imagine the Spirits of Great Writers Hovering Over You

When literary life is complicated and the right choice for one's writing seems unclear, I am often reminded of the night I went to hear Susan Sontag speak, about three years before her death. It was the December after 9/11. I had just started teaching at New York University School of Journalism. Those many months following the World Trade Center attacks found me in a blurry state. A chronic hacking cough kept me exhausted, and a chronic case of downtown panic kept my mind in a constant state of worry. Everyone in my West Village neighborhood seemed to be suffering from varying degrees of Post-Traumatic Stress Disorder. The existential anxiety and deep sadness was palpable in our lovely neighborhood, for months, and months.

At the end of 2001, the department sponsored a forum on "The Media's Response to 9/11."

Susan Sontag, essayist, novelist, activist, and icon, was one of the guest speakers. Days after 9/11, an essay she wrote for *The New Yorker*, critical of America, stood in sharp contrast to the patriotic stories that filled most of the other periodicals at the time. The right wing bashed her on *Nightline*, but she stood strong. A complex woman for complex times.

After talking about the politics of the day, Sontag opened up the floor for questions. Students lined up at the microphone, and one young undergrad asked her an eternal question about what inspires her to write. She responded with an answer for eternity.

She explained that when she sits down to write, even now (she was in her late 60s) she imagines that the writers she loved as a child—visionary poet William Blake, Tolstoy, Dostoyevsky, the great Russian writers are watching her. She told us that she feels a need to please them, to live up to their high expectations of her. She summoned Kafka, as a literary hero of hers, then, noted, "All writers love Kafka," which garnered a warm laugh of agreement from the audience.

Sontag was a fierce woman. I remember a few years later seeing her in the audience at a Fassbinder festival at the Film Forum. A few days later her piece on *The Marriage of Maria Braun* appeared in *The Village Voice*. I look at her as one of my heroes: eclectic, brilliant, and unapologetically individual. In this era where popularity trumps all, I particularly welcome her spirit when I write. Especially when I'm afraid. Especially when I can't decide which direction to take. I imagine her saying, "Make a decision. Stand by it. If you need to reverse yourself later—as I did with *On Photography*—then that is what you will do. But for now: write … with conviction, woman!"

If *you* are having trouble summoning up the courage to fully commit to a writing project, then summon up the advice of your literary heroes (dead or alive, and no I do not mean the fab '80s band who brought us "You Spin Me Round Like a Record"). Let your heroes lead you to a path of glory. (Note to self: talk to Stanley Kubrick's ghost tonight!)

Exercise: Literary Heroes

1. Conjure up the voice of one of your literary heroes, living or dead.

2. Write for five minutes using that voice to advise you as to what path to take.

3. If some other negative voice pops into your head (your ex, your Uncle Abel, your high school nemesis, a famous author you hate … whomever …), what would that voice say to pull you off track? Take a couple of minutes.

4. How would your hero defend you? Take a couple of minutes more.

5. If you are torn between projects, not sure which to write, what would your literary hero advise?

6. Briefly describe the "takeaway" advice you garnered from this exercise.

I asked a handful of clients and friends to try this method. Each adapted the exercise to his or her own style.

John McCaffrey is a well-published flash fiction/short story writer, who is finishing up a novel.

John

Here's a crack at the exercise (I'm riffing):

As I'm reading *War and Peace,* I'll let Old Tolstoy tongue-lash me (in English, but think Russian accent)…

You fool. You fool. You fool. Now that I said it three times, let me explain what I mean: you're a fool. This is not a disparagement on your character, your life outside the pen, but if you are indeed a writer (I speak of one who writes with their blood, not their fingers), what life is there but the pen? So without further cloaking my disdain for your predicament, your lament that your novel "gets wooden" (your words) with each passing edit, I say, simply, "good!" For what is wood but the foundation for homes, fuel for the fire, a club in the hand?

If your book is gaining solidity, then perhaps it needed solidity. The writer's mind is so curious that it questions its very essence. As long as you are engaged in the act, do not question the direction it takes you. If you were in a carriage and the horses pulling you along started to gallop, would you not rejoice at the expediency of getting to your destination faster? Conversely, say the beasts reduce their gait to a slow amble, might you not enjoy pushing your head out the window to take in the scenery? That is the trick for the writer to master, much like the magician whose showmanship is as vital as his sleight-of-hand: believe that your words are mesmerizing your readers, and they will. It is up to you to think yourself (as a writer) the fool, or be (as a writer) the fool. But I assure you the latter, if embraced with a blissful ignorance, will free you of the fool's shackles and let the pen in your hand dance.

Thank you Johnny and Leo! It is remarkable how free writers feel when given the opportunity to play. I think we can all "hear" the verve and grandiosity, the fun faux high-falutin' tone of John channeling one of the Russian greats (who is now undoubtedly hangin' out with Sontag, and therefore can hover over John when he needs him).

Hope Forstenzer's plays have been produced in New York City, and her glass-blowing work has been presented in Seattle shows. She was working on a screenplay when I asked her to partake in this game.

Hope

I have a sort of cycle of literary heroes, really. I don't usually imagine conversing with them, but I think if pressed I would talk to Haruki Murakami (I'd have to learn Japanese first). His attitude toward writing is both mystical and workmanlike. I think he would ask me which of the two I'd dreamed about, or have me think of each one individually and express the emotional responses, and he'd advise me to write the one that brought on the most intense feelings. When I'm feeling lost, Murakami would say not to worry, I think. He would say I should go do something I love to do—cook something very complicated, read a writer I love, exercise, go out and sit outside—and that the rest would take care of itself.

As for a negative voice, it would be Harlan Ellison for sure. I certainly don't hate him at all, but he's terribly harsh, and he would tell me to just sit down and write and write and write and stop whining.

I don't think Murakami would defend me himself. I think I would have to do it. That would probably be his way. I think I would say that not everyone writes the same way, and from my own experience I've learned that forcing it or thinking about it inevitably makes it worse, and letting it go for periods of time tends to take pressure off, and make things easier.

As for the "takeaway," it's this: seeking out ways to prevent anxiety from having an effect on any writing I do is important for any success I may have.

Daleth Carey Hall is a published nonfiction writer, currently at work on a novel.

Daleth

Tom Robbins would say, "There's a drumbeat of joy that wants to pound through you. There's a martini-shaped Poconos hot tub of joy that wants you to build it. It has been scientifically proven, through an experiment conducted with mole rats and college students in Spokane in 1968, that for every person who sets down the life their culture scared them into living and instead starts building whatever martini-shaped Poconos hot tub of joy their own soul has told them to build, the world as a whole becomes 0.2 percent better. I suggest you join that experiment."

Anaïs Nin would say, "Life shrinks or expands in proportion to one's courage. Treat this book like you treat your life— have courage." Oscar Wilde would say, "If you can't bear it, for goodness sake, have some wine and meet friends for dinner. One needn't give every night over to toil."

Tom Robbins would say, "Let the way find you. It's a writer, you're the pen. And it's older than you, not to mention at least three percent wiser, so you might as well give it a chance." Anaïs Nin would say, "Feel your way. Write in circles, in spirals …"

A negative voice might say, "I'm nervous, this is overwhelming, there's so much more I want to say and if I can't get it in, this won't be good enough."

To this, Tom Robbins would reply, "You can get it in, and if you can't, if it doesn't fit, it will fall to your feet and grow into some other story. That's okay. Let it fall, let it start growing into mushrooms around your feet—it'll take care of itself. You don't need to quit writing what you're writing to take care of it." Oscar Wilde would toss his hair with regal impatience and say, "Don't be ridiculous. The smallest part of what you have to say will still be greater than the entirety of what most others ever say."

Jennifer Neal, a writer, photographer, and former editor, is currently writing fiction.

Jennifer

If I were feeling lost and called upon them: Hunter Thompson would probably be drunk and stoned while imparting his advice and he might even dole out a pill or two. He would probably divert my attention by retrieving the shotgun and encouraging me to fire off a few rounds. God knows we all need a distraction and Scrabble just doesn't always cut it.

Edith Wharton would be more thoughtful and eloquent than Hunter. She's selfless enough to have gone to the front during the First World War to tend to soldiers. I want to say that she's more studious than Hunter, but that may not be true; Hunter was an avid reader, but he was also an avid TV watcher. I wonder what sort of role the television would have played in her life? Edith would probably tell me to revise and re-revise my plan, or indeed, draw up a schedule, and make my characters do exactly what they need to do in order to get to the end goal: possibly even tell me to use a timeline. I believe that Edith always had the end goal in mind. Plus, she reached out to people and friends, something that I've never done during my research. (I've just paraphrased them instead!) I would love to go back in time to meet Edith. She was a worldly adventuress at the time when most women had to stay at home and stab each other in the back.

You asked me to imagine a negative voice piping in with a put-down. This is a great question for an English person. English people don't need naysayers because they have each other. I come from a long line of naysayers. For example, when I had my first group photographic exhibition in Chelsea where I sold a couple of pieces, I called a friend in England and informed him excitedly. He responded: "You're not a bloody photographer! I'll take some pictures this weekend and you can stick those in, too!"

My ideal literary hero would tell me never to give up, and to ignore the naysayers and banish my judgment to England where it belongs. He would offer me new books to read and offer differing points of view and point out new opportunities.

Robin Gaines is a former journalist who recently completed a novel-in-stories.

Robin

My literary heroes are characters in books I love. I was lucky to have parents who read, so the house was stocked with gems. In junior high I was reading everything from Sidney Sheldon to Ernest Hemingway. From *Portnoy's Complaint* I learned about masturbation and Jewish guilt. Huck Finn and Scout Finch, racial prejudice. Holden Caulfield showed me how some kids mask their loneliness and sadness with humor, and Jay Gatsby proved that unrequited love feels the same for a 14-year-old (like me at the time) as it does for someone older. How can you not love these characters for giving you life lessons by example? And understanding, at least as much as humanly possible through words, what it was like to be in combat in Vietnam from the characters in *The Things They Carried* and *Going After Cacciato*. Ditto for World War I and II experiences in *All Quiet on the Western Front* and *The Naked and the Dead*. All better versions of military history than any textbook I ever muddled through in high school.

Well, you get the picture. The list goes on and on. And every reader's list probably includes their own favorite, nuanced, entertaining saints and sinners. As a writer, I am not unaware of the contribution we have to making these made-up individuals sing with aliveness. But like the puppeteer maneuvering the strings behind the scenes, good writers want the focus on what the puppets are doing and not the masterful finger work they are employing.

So when I am desperately trying to get to the core of the story and can't seem to find my way, I call upon my characters to show me the way. And they usually come to the rescue. I think because they're grateful to be out of my head, finally, and on the page. Exactly where they should be!"

Starr Goode is a literature professor and a well-published essayist.

Starr

Evelyn Waugh might say, "Look, you can't write a book just because you want to, just because you want to have a book. Like some Platonic pre-existing essence, whatever you want to write has to already be inside you before it can become an external, material form. A simple question connects you to what's waiting inside: 'What do you want?'"

I remember reading that Virginia Woolf, after hearing praise for T. S. Eliot's "East Coker" (from *The Four Quartets*), had to walk out over the marshes telling herself: "I am I; and must follow that furrow, not copy another." Even great geniuses can doubt themselves; I might not be much, but I am all I have, so why not give it a go?

Seema Srivastava, an art historian working on her first novel, used this exercise to ruminate on the question of "Which project should I work on?"

Seema

Oscar Wilde said, "We are all in the gutter, but some of us are looking at the stars ... go with the one that offers the potential of stars."

The challenge, of course, is to take this spirit of fun and "why not?" that tends to arise in these exercises, and apply that same spirit to your actual writing hours. Make it a game, not a chore.

As you can see, help from your literary heroes can be found anywhere and everywhere. But of course, despite your best efforts with these exercises, you may still have a voice in your head that calls out, "You're working on the wrong project!" Before you make any sudden moves, consider this: what if you pursue the project you committed to for a month, six weeks? When you've met your commitment you can work on whatever you like, ladybug!

Professional writers need to meet deadlines, and by sticking to your commitment you are increasing your level of professionalism.

That said, if you are so sure that you have another project that needs to be written *right now*, go for it. But know thyself, writer. If you wind up in the same ambivalent position in a month or two, you are going to have to admit that the problem lies within, and then bitch-slap yourself into reality. Do your hours. Bang the keys. Trust that the answers will come later. All writers, from Jack Kerouac to Raymond Carver, to working writers today and newbies alike, have struggled and will continue to struggle with these issues. You are in good company.

In a recent workshop, I read a little bit from a *New Yorker* magazine profile about the contemporary painter John Currin. Currin shared his view that the best work happens at the end. He felt that a big part of painting was not looking at one's paintings in progress too closely. He intimated that of course it doesn't look good now, but it will later.

Don't forget this is a garbage draft you are working on. You promised to make a mini-commitment (a matter of weeks) to this piece, in sickness and in health, for richer for poorer, and all the rest. Well, now's your chance to practice being a stand-up guy or gal. Maybe there's a reason the groom is not supposed to see the bride before the wedding. Maybe she's still working on her face! So avoid the temptation to judge these early pages before they are properly polished and dolled up. When in doubt, honor your commitment. Be your own hero.

Kudos, Kiddo(s)!

You grappled with the conflicting voices in your head and engaged with your literary heroes.

You showed some courage and verve and continued to commit to your project, your practice.

6

channel surfing

"Every moment new changes, new changes and new showers of deceptions to baffle and distract him."—Ralph Waldo Emerson

The fault lies not in our stars, but in ourselves, or perhaps more precisely, in our twenty-first-century addiction to staying plugged in! Like many of you, I feel great relief when I go to the country, far from the city, or to a foreign country, far from my home, and do not have access to e-mail and the Internet. As a writing coach, this is probably the number-one obstacle that my clients complain about. And I know how they feel.

As mentioned in Chapter 1, I used to be a Dictator. Absolutely rigid in my writing hours. Then I began to teach and no longer had the absolute freedom of a freelance writer. I went through a divorce and my home life changed; I found I had to take on more work to keep up with my newly doubled rent. I pursued a Master's in Creative Writing, which entailed being a student again, as well as a teacher. The result? I had to embrace the concept of multitasking. This was in 2005.

And to be quite honest with you, the multitasking was a great experiment for me. Like daily journalists who have to write amid the clackety-clack of other writers writing, and the hum of colleagues getting their stories by phone, I had to give up my precious, perfect writing time and write when I could with what I could. It was liberating to know that I could zoom in and focus for short periods on a particular story. It was empowering to see that I could finish one piece, get another one started, and work on the middle of a third piece.

But only a few short years later, the world has changed ... radically. Since the days of my first e-mail account back in 1996 (My screenname was SlickJilly, LOL!), the universe has sped up so fast that we not only have the distraction of e-mail or IMDB or Wikipedia; we now have blogs, YouTube, Twitter, Facebook, and on and on and on. And there's no sign that the infomania we all suffer from is going to abate any time soon. I am starting to feel nostalgic for the Y2K that could have been!

Using Meditation to Avoid Techno Addiction

Lee Siegel, another literary hero of mine, wrote a book titled *Against the Machine: Being Human in the Age of the Electronic Mob*, which I turn to for a taste of calm wisdom when I am feeling overwhelmed by all the white noise. Since his book's 2007 release, there have been more and more articles on this subject, but I believe he said it first and he said it best. Essentially, we are fast becoming a mean-spirited race of superficial idiots who are disconnected from each other and from ourselves, and can no longer distinguish between gossip and news! Ah, for the days when the TV was called "the idiot box" or "the boob tube." Talk about a gateway drug. (Hold on; I'm uploading a video of my dog breathing. I'll write more in a sec.)

Techno-addiction is an epidemic, for all of us today, but I think especially for writers, who, except for the rare old-worlders, all write on computers. Writers' retreats are great, but they are a luxury for the few. And even libraries, writers' spaces, and the like are all wireless now. So how does one fight the urge to check texts, read e-mails, and Google away those precious writing hours?

The answer, my dears, in four syllables: meditation.

The first time I meditated, I set an egg timer (five minutes was my goal), lit a candle, closed my eyes, and observed my breath, in and out, in and out. Ten seconds in: nothing! I was not a calm, blue ocean. I was flailing in a sea of neurotic thoughts. A few meditators had told me that a good way to connect with one's intuition was to stare into the flame and try to see it with the "third eye." Not the candle holder, but the actual flame. I had to open and close my eyes repeatedly before I could barely "see" the flame, its color, motion, and shape, in my third eye— the spot at the center area of my forehead.

Soon a switch flipped on. I observed my breath, and simultaneously a story started to form, like random puzzle pieces being tossed onto a dining room table that miraculously fit together. It began with an image. I saw myself taking my friend Paige out for practice driving lessons in Brooklyn. I felt as if I was watching a movie, or experiencing a dream. Then I heard the voice of my friend Scotty—a memory of our recent drive to Giants Stadium, to try and score Bruce tickets. I wove us in and out of Holland Tunnel traffic. "You're really queen of the merge," he said, impressed. (Though later that night he laughed at my parallel parking.) As I watched the dream-story of helping Paige learn to drive, I heard Scotty repeating his "queen of the merge" line in my head. Before I opened my eyes I saw an image of a David Wojnarowicz painting *Fever*, a response to the AIDS epidemic.

When the egg timer went off, I sat down and wrote a draft of a story called "Queen of the Merge." The writing experience felt very much like channeling. It all came out in one piece. Many of the elements from this brief meditation/channeling experiment ended up in the first draft; some were eventually discarded like a sheet of tracing paper.

But those were still the good old days. To combat the twenty-first-century compulsion to skim articles online, answer e-mails, update blogs, watch YouTube, and on and on … meditation seems like the best strategy. But when you can barely hold the thought "I ought to clear my mind and meditate" in your head before checking your voice-mail or sending a text, how in the world can you actually practice this free and freeing exercise?

Abdi Assadi, an acupuncturist friend and author of *Shadows on the Path*, treats a lot of writers and artists. "Writers tend to be really heady. Attentive, but in their heads when not writing. Common to all of them," so he advises, "They should start with five minutes a day. Every time the mind wanders, bring the focus back on breathing into the belly and feeling their bodies."

What Abdi speaks of is in the spirit of mindfulness meditation. Generally one sits on a cushion, spine straight (as if leaning against a strong tree), legs crossed, hands gently resting on the knees. In this position one closes the eyes and breathes naturally, focusing on each individual breath. Some silently say, "inhale, exhale." Inevitably, thoughts intrude on this simple process, usually followed by even more intrusive judgments over our inability to stay focused.

Larry Rosenberg advises in his book *Breath by Breath* to see the confused mental state that often arises during meditation not as an interference with your practice, but as your practice itself, your life itself, in that moment. He encourages people to examine those moments of confusion, so that ultimately they lead to clarity. For beginning meditators (and each time is a new beginning, a new breath, anyway), Rosenberg's book is a wonderful place to start.

Recently, I was working in my local writing space, suffering from what's known in meditation circles as "monkey mind" (hearing endless internal chatter as the brain jumps from one disconnected thought to the next). I felt gripped by an impossible-to-pin-down mix of worry, sadness, and confusion. I logged online to soothe myself, which only added guilt to the mix.

I put my head on my desk, and simply tried to focus on my breath. Painful feelings intruded, followed by amorphous troubled thoughts. I tried to observe them, the way one observes a character's mind while reading fiction. I was able to locate and "see" the emotions, the ideas that had spun out, and once observed they passed. My mood miraculously lifted! I logged off and began to write. It was not so different from the clear feeling one gets after a long swim. In this case, no country retreat or expensive gym membership was necessary!

Please note, I'm an eclectic meditator. Whatever works, that's what I do. My own experience can give you a sense of what works for me, but Insight Meditation is probably my technique of choice.

Insight Meditation tends to be geared toward "making note" of the feelings and perceptions that come up, while sitting: "feeling hungry," "feeling nervous." Breathe. Note. And don't judge. Translated to the techno-obsessive world of today, the equivalent might be, "Desperate to check e-mail." So be it! Don't torture yourself; just return to the breath. All of mindfulness meditation is aimed at staying in the present, with the breath, attuned to what is happening now (from an itch on your foot, to the sound of a car horn outside). When you find yourself drifting into a mental drama ("What if my story is moronic?"), return to the present.

Remember how creative you were as a child? How uninhibited about just playing and creating? That's what meditation can help you return to. The idea of the beginner's mind is to simply empty out all thoughts and attachment to what we (think we) know. Easier said than done, especially for brainy writers. One thing that has helped me, and a number of my writing clients, is to read books on the practice of meditation. There is something about the art of learning that appeals to almost all writers, and somehow, I've found, the knowledge can seep in and lead to a natural entry path to the "don't-know mind." Sounds like a Zen koan, doesn't it? In practical terms, if every Internet-addicted writer carried around a small meditation book (or just a Xeroxed article or chapter) as an antidote to the powers of the wireless connection we might end up getting a lot more writing done.

In their classic book *Insight Meditation*, Sharon Salzberg and Joseph Goldstein compare mindfulness to walking a tightrope: to maintain your balance on a tightrope you must focus on the moment, with steady concentration, and master the human tendency to compulsively seek pleasure/diversion, avoid unpleasant feelings, or (when feeling "okay") go on autopilot. The tightrope analogy illustrates that if something pleasant comes your way, you can't grab it lest you fall. If something unpleasant appears you mustn't pull away, or you could fall. You can't space out, or you might fall. The whole point is to pay attention, not spin out or space out in the mind. Salzberg and Goldstein's book also provides a perfect opening for a beginning meditation practice.

How Authors Use Meditation

Personally, I keep discovering more and more writers who do meditate or who desperately want to!

Writer Jim Savio (*The Fairy Flag and Other Stories*) told me, "I was initiated into Transcendental Mediation (mantra based) nearly 40 years ago. I never practiced it regularly, but would repeat my mantra in a variety of disquieting situations and true to my TM oath, I never revealed it. Later, my teacher invited all of us to make a six month, daily, half hour commitment to a meditation practice ... I fell headlong into it. Meditation helps me to focus, to concentrate—on my writing, my carpentry, my design work, my role as a husband and a father, my teaching. It has become essential, Jill, that's all I can say."

Avid meditator J. D. Salinger wove threads of Eastern thought into his Glass family novellas. And in "Teddy," from his *Nine Stories* collection, he provides a perfect illustration of "beginner's mind." The 11-year-old title character responds to a question about how he'd change the education system, by suggesting they get kids to empty out all the things they'd been told, including the idea that an elephant has a trunk. Instead the boy suggests showing the kids an elephant and letting them imagine what this great creature was, just as the great creature would have to assess what the little humans were.

Surrealist writers like André Breton were fond of Automatic Writing, now used in pretty much every writer's workshop, and simply called Free-Writing. Breton and co-conspirators like Leonora Carrington, Max Ernst, and Philippe Soupault put themselves into a "receptive frame of mind," and, of course, approached their automatic games with much creativity and mischief. *The Magnetic Fields* was the first collection of automatic texts.

Starr Goode, a recipient of The Henri Coulette Memorial Poetry Award from the Academy of American Poets, finds Metta (loving-kindness) meditations extremely helpful. She was referred by her acupuncturist to Insight Meditation author Salzberg, during a time of health crisis. The practice (which can be done anywhere) involves a repetition of four phrases to encourage Metta toward the self. None other than the Dalai Lama himself has "preached" showing compassion to the self first, and letting that compassion then spread out to others. For self-flagellating writers who tend to run to the strangely calming (and bitchy!) distraction of the Internet, rather than face the horror of our own snarky inner critics, spending five minutes a day on Metta practice could save you from the hours wasted trolling blogs and avoiding one's own work.

Dr. Nancy Williams, president of the Division of Psychoanalysis of the American Psychological Association and author of several psychology books, says, "I suspect that serious writers are fatally self-critical ... they have very high standards for themselves, and because of their sensitivity they live in fear of their own devastated reaction to negative evaluations of their work."

"Meditation helps one accommodate, a la Keats, a spacious doubt/unknowing, as opposed to the doubt that contracts and shuts down," says poet and Zen practitioner Genine Lentine, who collaborated with Stanley Kunitz on his last book, *The Wild Braid*.

Playwright Brooke Berman (*Hunting and Gathering*) meditates sometimes and practices Mysore Ashtanga yoga (which has a strong meditative component) four or five times a week. "The yoga, first thing in the morning, focuses my attention and helps me solve problems in the script. I find that my mental energy can only go so far in unlocking the characters and plot—I have to actually get the thing into my body so that the unconscious can engage on a deeper level with the core of the material. There are always meditation periods in yoga … I do find myself solving problems while I'm practicing, or receiving answers as to how to move forward."

My friend Claudia Valentino, an editor and writer for national magazine pieces shared these thoughts with me: "We don't need to get wrapped up in metaphysical definitions of the self in order to understand the relation between meditation and writing. Both grant greater access to that internal landscape which really is the source of everything we create. Writers need to be able to get there reliably and must believe that putting in uninterrupted, undivided time will make a qualitative difference in their work and in how they feel about it.

"If meditation is about anything it is about doing just one thing, one simple thing, well and without distraction. Writers won't find a better working model than that anywhere. Writers have always found ways to distract themselves and to avoid sitting down to face the page. But it must be granted that the Internet, and all that comes with it, is an amazingly insidious distraction. Writers need to know that, in this particular way, the work they do is different. Multitasking isn't for them."

Okay, Claudia, pretty straight talk. But what am I going to tell all my Facebook friends?

"I also recommend a tiny but extremely awesome book," Claudia said. "*Zen Mind, Beginner's Mind*, by Shunryu Suzuki-Roshi. He helped found the first Zen monastery in the United States: Tassajara in northern California. I can say that this slim volume will fit beautifully into your life, will not overwhelm you, or take up too much house room. It's deep."

The 5 Ws of journalism could help you to clear your mind and find your best story.

Exercise: Channel Surfing

Like homeopathic medicine, channel surfing takes the poison (mindless surfing) and transforms it into the cure (finding and focusing on one subject you connect to). It is not meant to compare with traditional meditation but simply meant to help a writer peaceably collaborate with the imagination.

Five steps, five fingers:

1. Sit

Adopt a comfortable sitting position, close your eyes, observe your breath.

2. Count

Step two is meant to simply warm up your writing fingers. (No coincidence I came up with this when I began playing piano!) Count from one to five on your left hand and back down, five to one, on your right. Breathe in deeply from one to five while focusing on the left hand, and breathe out using the right. Count and tap (sans sound) as if you are warming up to bang

the keys of a typewriter. If that distracts, just gently press the
pads of your fingers into your knees or thighs. Find your own
pace.

3. Surf

As you count, allow images, thoughts, and phrases to sift
through your consciousness. Just as you might surf the net
or click the remote, allow your mind to move speedily
through its storehouse of information, imagination, and
mental garbage. When you click onto something—an image,
a phrase—that grabs you: focus. Attempt to see or hear it
more clearly.

4. Question

Continue to silently tap fingers, but now replace counting
numbers with counting the five mantra-like words as follows.... Use each finger to correspond with the "5 Ws" of
journalism (and all classic storytelling): Who? What? Where?
When? Why? Don't try and answer these questions. This is
not about work right now; it's about repetition of words, just
as a moment ago it was about repetition of numbers, repetition of breath. Silently repeat each of the Ws as you tap a
corresponding finger. If you prefer, you can also just repeat
one of the words until you are ready to move on to the next,
like this: "Who?", "Who?", "Who?" ... (At first you may feel like
Woodsy the Owl, the character behind the phrase, "Give a
Hoot, Don't Pollute," but trust me, that'll wear off soon!)

5. Write

At the end of five minutes, write for five minutes (or more!)
using whatever came up in the meditation as a jumping-off
point. Without thinking, focus on the strongest story, idea,
image, or line that came to you during your practice and
identify the 5 Ws—now, on the page.

Hopefully all that tapping will help you to tap in! And remember, different meditation styles work for different writers, just like any other writing-related support. As Brooke Berman says, "I was never going to be one of those old-school writers who could sit down with a scotch and a cigarette. For one thing, I don't drink scotch, and for another, I've never smoked. But the breath and a cup of a coffee? And mindfulness? It totally works for me."

Indeed! Brooke, a successful, award-winning off-Broadway playwright is a lovely example of old school meets new school. She is prolific and serious about her craft, but is also very plugged in to the modern world.

Writers today are really not allowed the luxury of, as my mother would say, "sitting in a garret." We have to get our work done, but simultaneously, in very erratic, uncertain times, we as artists also need to tend to the commerce parts of our career. The Internet is where a lot of networking and marketing takes place, and I don't know any working writers who have the luxury of sitting back and just letting publishers find their work, and then letting the publishing houses do the work of selling their books. *Everyone* is simply too busy. And we live in a multitasking world, although I wish it weren't so.

That said, I believe a little cup o' mindfulness can be mastered in any moment. All mindfulness entails is checking in with yourself and reconnecting. Ironic, because all the cyber-connecting we do inevitably puts us out of touch with ourselves. I know you're busy and need to get online right now, so here are some quickies! And please be aware, although there is no direct connection to your writing in these mini-meditations, they will help to clear your mind so that you can stop your mind from racing and your fingers from scrolling the mindless web chatter, and you can actually *get some writing done*. Begin the sanity!

In the time it takes to cook an egg, you can connect to your true self.

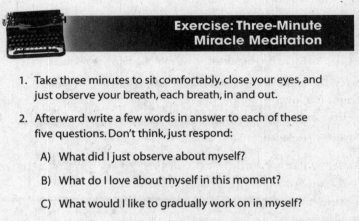

Exercise: Three-Minute Miracle Meditation

1. Take three minutes to sit comfortably, close your eyes, and just observe your breath, each breath, in and out.

2. Afterward write a few words in answer to each of these five questions. Don't think, just respond:

   A) What did I just observe about myself?

   B) What do I love about myself in this moment?

   C) What would I like to gradually work on in myself?

   D) What part of my body do I need to be extra in tune with?

   E) What's the overall message of responses A–D combined?

Get out of your head and on your feet.

Exercise: Moving Meditation

1. Turn off the computer and take a 10-minute walk outside, but with the intention of moving slowly.

2. Turn your attention to each step, the lifting of your foot, the touching down to ground.

3. Don't think of this as physical exercise, but as an exercise in mindfulness.

Mindfulness, made even easier.

Exercise: Free Your Mindfulness (and the rest will follow)

1. Sit comfortably.

2. Close your eyes.

3. Focus on your breath for a minimum of five minutes.

4. When the mind wanders (it will!) return to the breath.

5. Observe your emotional state: what are you feeling and where in your body are you feeling it? What is the tangible experience of that emotion like?

6. Ride the wave of those feelings; stay with them and breathe through them.

Sometimes called "metta meditation," this could help your endorphins to flow.

Exercise: Peace Training

1. Sit comfortably, close your eyes, and follow your breath (as above!) for five minutes, and while you do this:

2. Send a short mantra of love ("may you be safe and at peace") to, for example …

   A) Yourself.

   B) Your loved ones.

   C) The benign people in your life.

   D) The negative people who cause you angst.

Kudos, Kiddo(s)!

So many kudos, so little time!

You tapped into your ability to meditate, any time, any place. You can now do this when your kids are screaming, your e-mail message icon is blinking, your head is pounding, etc. This is major, all because it is focused on the minor: the moment you are experiencing right now.

You found a new way to scan your overloaded brain for ideas. You can "channel surf" when you are in between projects and seeking inspiration, or right now, when you are engaged in a project, but need to figure out, "What do I want to write today?"

Congratulations! You have finished Step One and are now ready for … (deep breath please): Step Two!

step 2

arrange

Arrange your story into a concrete shape.

7

medium ... well?

Congratulations! You've survived Step One. You were able to come up with an idea and commit to it, without having to commit yourself to a mental hospital. (Wish I could say the same. You have no idea the toll this work takes on me, darlings!)

Before you pop open the bubbly, though, might I gently suggest you *get your butt in the chair and listen to me!*

All right, now that I've gotten your attention again, here's what we need to focus on.

In order to bring your work to fruition in the real world, you need to find the right shape, the right container to hold your story in. Don't run out to Boxes-R-Us just yet. That's not what I mean.

Choosing Your Medium

First you need to validate for yourself what is the *medium* for your tale. Screenplay? Novel? Essay? Short story? Poem? Play? Or perhaps down the road you will do all of the above, or live to see your work elevated or commercialized by an adaptation in another form.

Author Ray Bradbury began writing "Bright Phoenix" in 1947; it was published as a novella in *Galaxy Science Fiction* in 1951. The story further evolved into *Fahrenheit 451*. Like George Orwell's *1984* and Aldous Huxley's *Brave New World*, Bradbury's dystopian tale of a book-burning society quickly became a popular hit and becomes more and more relevant every year.

The author himself, however, was compelled to play with its form long after the novel was published in 1953 and achieved international success. Many years later he adapted *Fahrenheit 451* into a play. Some of the significant changes in the theatrical version seem influenced by Francois Truffaut's film adaptation of the novel, released in 1966. It's also been adapted by others for radio, and even video games! Another film adaptation may be in the works as well.

Though the obsession with the story continues, and may soon be developed to fit other mediums, Bradbury himself has said that his original inspiration for the novel was his love of books themselves.

Recently, I saw a production of *Fahrenheit 451* by a Brooklyn-based theater company. My friend Maya Ciarrocchi, a visual artist, created the visual design for the performance. She came to my New York University arts journalism class to discuss the show, before the students went to see it. One of her more interesting challenges, she told us, was figuring out a way to create a visual replication of Bradbury's electronic hound. The hound was a key element in the novel and in the play. But apparently Truffaut did not want the hound to appear in the film; this was a source of frustration for the author.

Truffaut got his way; film, after all, is a director's medium. In a novel, the author controls all. In experimental theater ... well, you tell me! Adaptations can teach us a lot about what form works best for what type of story. Some stories can work beautifully, if differently, in all types of mediums. Yet always the question of what can be included, what should be excluded must be asked.

Notes on the Various Mediums

You may want to consider the intrinsic nature of each medium while deciding which one is right for your piece. Consider the following questions.

- Long or short form?

  The benefit of the long form is you have room to tell a larger story. How big is the story you want to tell? If it involves several characters, think long. The short form allows you to focus on the micro. The tiny moments in which things, relationships, change. The reader or audience experience the piece in a kind of close-up. Intimacy is key in the short form.

  Exceptions: *My Dinner with Andre* has the intimacy of a conversation between two friends (in fact that's the whole narrative), yet it is a full-length movie. The length works, in my opinion, because the subject matter of the conversation is so varied, expansive, and worldly. If the men only discussed one concrete incident, the audience might get bored. Many did! But for those who love this film, the love is a passionate one.

- Fiction or nonfiction?

Prose writers, who all, to a degree, draw from real experience *and* use their imaginations, must ask themselves if their story has more power when told through clear but meaningful exploration of the truth, or through the creation of situations and characters that are imagined. In the latter case you are not tied to the facts. In the former case, the facts must be selected and sequenced carefully, for maximum impact on the reader.

- Play or screenplay?

Dialogue plays a key role in both forms, but a play is essentially the playwright's medium; dialogue is almost everything. In film, everything must be visualized.

There are numerous exceptions, and many other forms, but if you can ruminate on the above three questions, you will get much closer to understanding which medium is the right one for your piece.

I asked my writing buddy, Wendy Jo Cohen, an award-winning independent filmmaker, to share some advice on how to decide on the appropriate medium for your writing project. Over the years, she has been a great help to me, and to my workshoppers, with literary matters such as these.

After getting Wendy's initial thoughts on form, I checked in with our mutual friend Matthew Howe for his input. Matt is the author of the memoir *Film Is Hell* and his horror fiction has been widely published.

And full disclosure: in the late 1980s, while attending the State University of New York at Purchase, Wendy and I made an 18-minute film called *You Dirty Scum;* Matt filmed it. Wendy and I play street ruffians Frankie and Joey, respectively. We also double as ourselves, two pretentious filmmakers dissecting the story of the urchins. It's out there. It may be on my website. It's not pretty. Okay, I feel better now. Let's listen in! Think of this as a dialogue; there is no absolute answer my friends or yours can provide you with, but Wendy and Matt certainly raise questions, and suggest approaches that you should consider.

Point Counterpoint

Wendy: The material usually tells you what it wants to be. But then there's the issue of which form the writer is most comfortable working in. A writer who is torn as to which way to go should probably think about why they want to tell the story, how they want to tell it, and then think about what each form has to offer.

Is the fact that something really happened the most important thing? If so, you'd go with memoir. Then of course, you need to stick with the facts. If you want to take something that really happened but go further with it ... use it as a leaping-off point only, then a novel would be a good bet.

If you want to have room for interior life—the characters' thoughts and analysis about what is happening while it is unfolding—you want to stay away from the screenplay because there is very little room for that sort of thing. If your story is primarily action-oriented and visual, then a screenplay is appropriate. If someone really has a hankering to use beautiful or poetic language, it is pretty much wasted in a screenplay because the only language that will end up on screen is the dialogue.

There are certain storytelling techniques that are cinematic in nature (i.e.: visual), and if that is how you write then you would be well off in that form. When you read Dickens, you get the sense that the guy would have been a screenwriter had movies existed at that time. It's the way he reveals things visually, uses "jump cuts" and extreme changes in point of view (visual point of view, that is). He also paints an entirely visual atmospheric picture with his descriptions. You really get the sense of watching a movie. Robert Lewis Stevenson does a similar thing, although not quite at the level of Dickens. So it is possible to write a cinematic piece of literature, but I would say that it doesn't work as well in the other direction. That is, literary screenplays usually aren't so good. I'm currently reading *Treasure Island,* by the way. You can see why they made that into a movie ... two times.

Matt: I agree with Wendy, but I want to add a few thoughts. First of all, I've done adaptations both from screenplay to novel and vice versa. I would really urge young writers to write either novels or memoirs. Novels give you access to one tool that screenplays don't: getting inside the character's head. That was a lesson I learned as I wrote my first novel first as a script, then tried to adapt it to novel form. I saw what was missing ... basically the entire book! That's because I was totally outside my character.

Screenplays are notoriously difficult to write. There are much more rigid principles of structure and length. You also have a more limited canvas. Plus, and perhaps most importantly, no one can really appreciate a screenplay until it is turned into a movie. And let's hope that in the process, it is not utterly destroyed. A novel, on the other hand, can be printed or e-mailed, and enjoyed by anyone who can read.

Novels and memoirs can stand alone. A screenplay is really just a blueprint for someone else to work from. Yes, there are cases when a story is best suited for the screen. In this case, I would still advise writing the story as a novel. If you then wanted to go forward and adapt the story for the screen, you'd have all that work you've done, getting inside the character's heads, to back up your script and make it that much richer.

Wendy: I agree entirely about how difficult it is to write a screenplay because of the points cited. I had to write my film as prose first. I have 200 pages of prose that helped me figure the whole thing out. If I could stand to do any more work in this world, I would go back and flesh those 200 pages out into a decent novel. There is so much richness to the story I wrote as prose, unfortunately there was no way I could put into the film. There are definitely natural born screenwriters, but those people wouldn't be asking themselves the question (which do I write?) in the first place.

Matt: All during my days as a low-budget action filmmaker, I was writing short stories. My crazy idea was that I might break free of film bondage through writing! I sort of lost momentum at one point. Then I quit the company I was working for and went back to freelancing. I wanted to write, but felt empty of ideas. I was also haunted by the low-budget film experience, it really messed me up, mentally, financially, and career-wise.

I told the stories from my shoots to people on set, and everyone laughed their butts off. I started talking about writing a memoir. It was my buddy Steve, a sound guy, who finally said 'You should just do it, man. Just do it. Do it.' And I did it, and am still doing it.

As for short story versus novel, here is a case where the material really does dictate. I have definite "story" ideas, which are small little nuggets, and I have "novel" ideas that are larger and more sprawling. Sometimes a story idea will blossom into a novel, but I find I just know which type of idea I'm onto almost from the moment it first forms in my head. Probably not much help. I'd say start writing and see where it takes you. But never pad or stretch!

I shared Wendy and Matt's thoughts with you because so many writers who've come my way have worked on both prose and screenplays. These questions about form though, are eternal.

Stay Flexible

In 1956 Marion Capron interviewed Dorothy Parker for *The Paris Review* (the full interview is posted on the magazine's website). At the time, Parker was living with her beloved poodle in a midtown Manhattan hotel. She was asked whether she thought her verse-writing was any benefit to her prose. "Franklin P. Adams once gave me a book of French verse forms and told me to copy their design, that by copying them I would get precision in prose. The men you imitate in verse influence your prose, and what I got out of it was precision, all I realize I've ever had in prose writing."

Parker also wrote plays and screenplays, and Capron asked her if she ever tried the novel form. "I wish to God I could do one," she replied. "But I haven't got the nerve. I'm trying now to do a (short) story that's purely narrative. I think narrative stories are the best, though my past stories make themselves stories by telling themselves through what people say. I haven't got a visual mind. I hear things. But I'm not going to do those he-said, she-said things anymore, they're over, honey, they're over. I want to do the story that can only be told in the narrative form, and though they're going to scream about the rent, I'm going to do it."

Exercises: Shape Shifting

1. Write three paragraphs synopsizing your story, for one of the forms you are considering. (For example, "in the non-existent [on this planet] play *Who Ordered the Meat Loaf?*, Don, an aging exterminator and former child star, confesses to his wife, Suspiria, that he is sick of his life among the bugs ..."). Do the same for the next medium you are considering. (Example: "In the [never before written] memoir *From Rug Rat to Bug Batterer,* the narrator takes us through his experiences as a semi-famous child star through his degradations as an anonymous 'Bug Man.' In part one of the book, we begin at the end, when Don gives notice to his father, who owns the exterminating company ..."). Do this for as many mediums as you are seriously considering. After, ask yourself: "Which sounds the most natural?"

2. For each medium you are considering, write a page in which you rave about all the exciting aspects of writing in that form. For instance, what is it about telling your story in the form of a novella (a work of fiction, average range: 20,000–50,000 words) that thrills you? Now write a page describing all the negatives to writing in this form. Afterward, write one sentence encapsulating your final thoughts (pro and con) for each medium. (Example: "I have always wanted to write a novel, and this story is big enough, yet intimate enough to be the one; on the other hand, I fear I may get lost in the middle, having never written in this form before.")

3. Choose one scene from the middle of your story and write it in each form that you are considering. In which form does it seem the most compelling?

4. Outline your story in each form you are wondering about (try a 10 bullet point outline). Which outline has the strongest narrative momentum?

5. Meditate for five minutes. (See Chapter 6.) Afterward, ask, "Which form should I write this story in?" Still unsure? Write down each medium on a scrap of paper. Throw the papers into a hat and pick one. You can't decide? Then the hat decides for you, baby! Seriously, many great artists have followed the chance method. Why not?

If you are still not absolutely sure of the medium, worry not. Go forward. If you choose screenplay and later discover that the true form is a novel, I have no doubt you will be able to use all that rich dialogue when you make the switch to prose. Conversely, all the deep character work you did on your novel won't be for naught when you are forced to compress your work into subtext for a movie script.

Many of my favorite writers have expressed themselves in a myriad of mediums. Playwright Arthur Schnitzler wrote *Traumnovelle*, also known as *Dream Story*, a short novel about the complexities of marriage, later made into Stanley Kubrick's final masterpiece of a film, *Eyes Wide Shut*. Jorge Luis Borges was wildly experimental in his fiction and masterfully transparent in his nonfiction. James Agee wrote the text for the sprawling nonfiction epic *Let Us Now Praise Famous Men*, which was accompanied by the iconic photographs of Walker Evans; he also wrote the soulful novel *A Death in the Family*, along with the screenplay for the Hollywood gothic *The Night of the Hunter*, plus books of letters and a great deal of wise and witty journalism and film criticism. Delmore Schwartz wrote poetry and short fiction with equal doses of compassion. He, too, was a respected critic, and worked for many years on an ambitious play called *Genesis*.

What do all of these writers have in common? They're dead! So while you are still breathing, thinking, and feeling, pick a medium and write within its boundaries, baby. Break the boundaries if you need to.

Kudos, Kiddo(s)!

You explored the methods of different mediums.

You chose a medium for your piece.

These are no small feats. And I promise: your feats won't fail you now!

8

navigating the narrative

Now that you know what you are writing (screenplay, memoir, novel, story, etc.), you are going to have to figure out the form of your story, the genre. Come back here! I've locked the doors and microchipped you. There is no escape, you coward!

Discovering Your Structure

Every piece of writing has its own spine, its own natural structure. Perhaps you are writing a family saga, and you sense that what you really need is to tell the story as a novel, and from multiple points of view, over many generations. Or maybe you want to write a humorous, informative standalone essay on the cultural history of tube socks.

Like a painter, I suggest you begin with broad strokes. Start "painting" on the page, with words, and see where this takes you. At this stage of writing, it's natural to want to control the minutiae. What's more effective, however, for most writers, is to work up the courage to make some bold moves. It's those moves that will reveal the whole to you, and make the polishing of your prose, the tightening of your transitions that much easier *later.*

In the beginning, it is usually a good idea to just get that garbage draft down on the page. But at some point, if you have a short story that is heading toward 100 pages, or a novel that is coming up on 1,000, you may want to consider pinning down your structure so that it can hold your narrative.

So what kind of structure would be best for your literary baby?

Dostoyevsky mastered the rant in *Notes from the Underground.* Dreiser wrote a long workmanlike narrative to support the working boy's journey in *An American Tragedy.* Cassavetes's film script for *Shadows,* his first movie, reads like a jazz album/beat poem.

The structure of your piece should reflect its personality, its DNA.

So what are the various types of structures? I've gathered and given my spin on a dozen key narrative strategies for you to study, experiment with, and master. What follows is an eclectic mix of classic forms and a handful of kooky takes on narrative that I've culled from my years as a writer, as a coach, and (more than anything) as a reader. Of course there are more, but this should give you plenty to start with. Sometimes structures overlap, but let's not overcomplicate this chapter, righto, old chap? Structure Immersion class begins now!

A Crash Course in Narrative

Hero's Journey

Joseph Campbell, scholar of mythic forms, is the expert on this form. And the Charlie Kaufman film *Adaptation* sends it up brilliantly. Many books have been written about this type of narrative, but if you think of Dorothy's journey from the farm through the magical terrain of Oz all the way back to Kansas, with lessons learned and character tested along the way, you are definitely halfway home.

Tale

Graham Greene described his works as "entertainments." *The Third Man* and *The Quiet American* were made to be adapted into films because they were such delicious yarns. A tale often has the feeling of an escapade, but as Greene's work proves, a tale can be incredibly deep, well-crafted and literate, as well as entertaining. O. Henry mastered the form in so many of his stories. Remember "The Gift of the Magi"? A tale has a mythic quality. It may be grounded in realism but there is often a quality of adventure to it that gives it a more imaginative flavor.

Missive

This could be the diary, journal, or blog form. A letter, e-mail, or memo missive is another possibility. And I think of the rant as a close relation of this structure. From Alice Walker's epistolary novel *The Color Purple* to Fyodor Dostoyevsky's diatribe novel *Notes from the Underground*, this structure allows the reader to see the mechanics of a very subjective narrator's mind. Many of J. D. Salinger's fictional story/novellas about the Glass family are written as letters or monologues. Here, voice is everything.

Epic

Sprawling is the word that comes to mind. An epic has grand aspirations; it must hold a *big* story. The narrative is conventional in structure in that the hero, as in the hero's journey model, has a clear goal and is determined to meet it, no matter how tough the challenges. Warren Beatty's 1981 film *Reds* is a good example. Love. War. Communism. And the first film I ever went to see that had an intermission! Gabriel Garcia Marquez brings magical realism to the epic form.

World of

Another kind of sprawl, but this time much less linear, and much more rambling in form; digressions abound, and often we get into more than one character's head. One of my favorite books, John Irving's *The World According to Garp,* and many of Charles Dickens's novels are examples of this generous, big-spirited form. (No coincidence that Irving cites Dickens as a writing hero.) More modern writers such as David Foster Wallace in *Infinite Jest* have taken this form. And John Cassavetes has done films that have a "World of" feel, such as *Faces* and *A Woman Under the Influence*. There is often a feeling of deep compassion that emanates from this form of storytelling. Epic plays? How about Tony Kushner's *Angels in America*?

Collection

The key word for this form is complementary. Nella Larsen's *An Intimation of Things Distant,* two novellas from the Harlem Renaissance period, are the perfect complement to each other, making *Quicksand* and *Passing* into a two-for-one double the fun experience. David Sedaris's humor essay collection *Holidays on Ice* are all connected by the theme of the Christmas season. Walt Whitman's *Leaves of Grass* is of one piece, though it contains many glorious poems. Alan Lightman's *Einstein's Dreams* is an experimental collection of interconnected stories, comprised of fictional explorations of the famous title character at different points in time.

Single Form

This could be a single essay. A single short story. A single poem. Its strength is in its precision, its smallness, its desire to be perfect and complete but unassuming, like that first cup of coffee in the morning. Think Gay Talese's essay "Frank Sinatra Has a Cold" or John Cheever's story "Goodbye, My Brother."

Love Story

So much can be said of this familiar form, so here I will say little: a romance is at the center of what drives this structure. With obstacles. Often a love triangle.

Traveler's Tale

This structure feels less personal and personality-driven than the Hero's Journey model, though both are focused on journeys. The Traveler's Tale is much more focused on literal place, or places. The Hero's Journey is often metaphorical. When organizing a Traveler's Tale, think of literally mapping out the route of the protagonist. *On the Road* by Jack Kerouac is a great model of the Traveler's Tale. And for a more precise map, V. S. Naipaul's *Area of Darkness* travels well, as does Paul Bowles's *The Sheltering Sky*.

The Question

This form has a very cerebral, philosophical feeling to it. Short stories like "Borges and I," by Jorge Luis Borges—which poses the question, "What is identity?"—and novels like *The Unbearable Lightness of Being* by Milan Kundera—which poses the question, "Which type of romantic relationship is more satisfying, a light one or a heavy one?"—are great examples. Philip Roth's *The Plot Against America* poses a penetrating historical "what if" question. In narrative nonfiction, Oliver Sacks is a master of this form, which is basically an exploration of a question. Unless you are being purposely didactic, it is wise to follow the path of your question without trying to guide the text toward some absolute (read: boring) conclusion.

The Musical Composition

This is a structure that is very rhythmic; it could literally be the book for a musical that mirrors in its structure the type of musical it aims to be—for example, operatic like *Rent* or decadent like *Cabaret*. But a quiet book like Michael Cunningham's short novel *The Hours* is a good example of an elegantly composed structure. The chapters alternate between the points of view of the characters (all connected to Virginia Woolf), and the structure is spare and elegant, the perfect container for such a lovely, soulful story. Many authors are musicians or music aficionados themselves (Bang the Keys!) and musical footprints can be found in their work, from Thomas Mann to Haruki Murakami.

Hybrid/Experimental

This may be a blend of fact and fiction, a game of sorts, like Julio Cortazar's novel *Hopscotch*. Remember, the experimental structure can be anything, but the author must discover and then be able to articulate to himself the rules of his game!

There was a beautiful piece called "Micro Stories" in a recent *Harper's* magazine. Author John Edgar Wideman compiled a series of "flash fiction" (very, very short) pieces to create one textured story that was quite moving.

Dante structured his epic poem *The Inferno* to mirror the narrator's nightmare tour through the nine circles of hell; James Merrill's epic poem *The Changing Light at Sandover* is structured to reflect the true mystical and social experiences he and his artist friends shared while performing séances with a Ouija board. Max Frisch constructed his novella *Man in the Holocene* using lists and cut-outs from the encyclopedia to provide us with a map of associations to better understand Geiser, the lonely, learned protagonist. In J. M. Coetzee's novel *Elizabeth Costello* the title character gives a series of lectures, mainly on animal rights, which gives the book a feeling of a powerful nonfiction foundation.

The key to structure is containment. Your story, by nature, is limited. Even *The Neverending Story* had an ending! In *Poetics*, Aristotle wrote, "… a whole is that which has beginning, middle, and end." How you arrange the three, and how you micro-arrange the parts within, is up to you; you are master of your literary universe. That amount of power can be intoxicating, daunting, and a whole lotta fun.

I think I learned the most about structure when I was working hard on an essay titled "The Rehearsal Man" (an expanded version of "The Rehearsal Man" can be found on my website: www.bangthekeys.com), which was first published in *Lilith* magazine. I spent about five months working on this piece, and it was only a handful of pages. My aim was to create a "rela-tionship resumé." I created this structure early in the essay's development; I'd never seen this form before and I was excited by its built-in limitations. I used my invention of a "relationship resumé" to try to explore a particularly disturbing pattern in my romantic history. It was clear, from the beginning, that the key to the essay's success would be concision. I needed to be as pre-cise and clear as if I were writing a real resumé.

The structure did appear in my imagination like a gift, but it was my friend Angela Patrinos who helped me to polish the prose and make sure that every word had earned its place in each sentence. Angela's story "Sculpture 1" had been published in *The New Yorker*, and anthologized in *Nothing But You: Love Stories from the New Yorker*, alongside Raymond Carver, John Cheever, Mary Gaitskill, and many other impressive authors, and I knew she had exacting standards.

But before she could extract a hardcore line edit out of me, I had to throw down the prose in those broad strokes; I worked the structure first, the lines second. Because the structure was so solid I was able to take it when Angela confronted me about an awkward sequence within a paragraph; that sequence threw the structure off. Of course, after listening to her hammer away at my piece I did scream (more than once): "I want to throw you through a plate glass window—twice!" It didn't come to that, but only because the structure was sound (even if my mind was not).

Exercise: Quickies to Uncover Artful & Charming Keys to Structure

Yes, dear ducky, the acronym for these little exercises is indeed …

"Quacks"

Now stop dilly-dallying and lolly-gagging and sally forth to do your Quacks!

1. Okay, quacky, load up your weapon with bullets! By bullets I mean the same kind of quick phrases or sentences that you would use in a work memo. Bullet out in 8 to 12 plot points the structure of a favorite book, film, story. Try to adapt your piece to a similar structure.

2. What is the essential conflict of your story? Write two full pages discussing it. Then pare what you wrote down to one page. Then half a page. A paragraph. A sentence. A word.

3. Bullet out your structure in six bullets using an unusual structure, one that does not seem like a natural fit for your piece. (Example: you are writing a love story; bullet it out like it's an essay, or a courtroom transcript.) See if there is

anything you can use from this counterintuitive structure to help you to nail down an outline for your piece.

4. Speaking of outlines … write one for your piece. Screenwriters call 'em "treatments," a novelist must write a synopsis. It's all the same idea. One page. Outline your story. Just the story—as in what happens, and in what sequence. From that narrative page, pull out the "bullets" and use them as a shorthand guide as you work on your story.

5. Write out a clear question asking fellow writers for help with your structure. Example: "I am working on a short story about a corrupt politician on his way to his teenage daughter's funeral; I want to include flashbacks from their relationship but don't know where to place them." Toss that question out at your writing group, on your social networking site, or e-mail it to a select cabal of comrades. Offer to help them in return, of course.

Structure Spills Over

In focusing on the arrangement of narrative, the spine, the structure, a funny thing starts to happen. One starts to notice a yearning for structure in real life, too. The structure can be wild. It hardly has to be early to bed early to rise, but a sense of method, of order, of organization inevitably starts to spill out into one's real life. And that's when you know you are on the right track and that you should stay on track.

Kudos, Kiddo(s)!

You have experimented and a found a form that just might work for your piece. This is a huge milestone.

9

your hero ain't nothin' without a P.L.O.T.W.I.C.H.

I've been coaching writers for many years, and readers, I must confess: workshop after workshop, plot is the subject that is most likely to make people break out in hives and run screaming from the room. Although a small percentage of writers are masters of plot, most suffer from plot-phobia. I can empathize. I myself am a character-as-destiny type (also the name of the band I co-founded with Beyoncé back in the day ... Beyoncé Esther Finklebaum, that is).

When I was preparing for a workshop in which the theme was "plot," I sent a note out to my writer friends, asking for any tips they'd like to share with my students. Interestingly, the three I heard back from were all movie people. You already heard from Wendy and Matt in Chapter 7. Well, they piped in with thoughts on this subject as well, as did Chris Downey, a writer and producer on *The King of Queens*. I've actually known Chris since we met in high school ... in Queens. When I asked Chris for his advice on plot, he'd just recently sold his screenplay *My Beautiful Coma* to New Line Cinema, and since then has gone on to co-create the TNT series *Leverage*, starring Timothy Hutton.

I thought it was telling that the three folks who responded were all basically film people. Clearly, plot and structure are the bacon and eggs of their business, but also I think you can tell by their responses that these are folks who think about the question, "How can I build a better narrative?" all the time. If you are indeed working on a film script, you could get some literal help from my friends. And if you are working on prose, their advice may help you to get out of the Me Talk Pretty One Day syndrome, and help you to actually focus on the narrative momentum of the *story*.

See what wisdom you can cull from the bits of Chris, Matt, and Wendy's structure advice that resonate for you. We will meet on the other side to do some exercises, my friends! In the meantime, excuse me while I brew a cuppa joe.

Chris on Plot: "Break it Down"

In TV and film, I don't go by a lot of the screenwriting tomes. For example, in film I don't think in terms of a 30 page first act, a 60 page second act and a 10 to 20 page third act. I think of a film in terms of segments, each with a beginning, a middle, and an end, that are linked together in some way. I think I came to this more as a way to trick myself into believing the project was not so daunting. You know, "Oh, a movie is just three 30-page stories? You mean, three sitcom episodes? That's a breeze." But I also think that it makes for a better movie. You won't get a sense that you're spinning your

wheels for an hour in the middle if there are two distinct stories happening, one right after the other. The trick, of course,
is not to resolve the main issue on page 60.

I do believe that the two most important things to do when
setting out to write a film (or play or any other fiction) is to
know what the main character wants and to make him (or
her) active in trying to achieve it in every single scene. The
easiest of these "wants" is external. Jack wants the suitcase.
But even if it's emotional—Jack wants to get over the death
of his child—it's still a drive. When I read scripts that don't
work for me, it's generally because it's not clear what the
main character wants or he's just standing around watching
things happen to him. This is my big problem with a lot of
independent films and modern fiction. A bunch of rich kids
grappling with their growing disillusionment in post-9/11
New York is not a story to me. They need a suitcase.

I know that sounds glib, but if you look at things that have
mass appeal and longevity, they all have active characters,
with a clear-cut goal and a lot of plot. *Seinfeld,* the *Law and
Order* shows, Cherry Jones's nun character in the play *Doubt,*
if you want an example from the legit theater world. (Meryl
Streep plays the Sister role on the big screen.)

A lot of people start out a project with a character. "She's
a neurotic single gal trying to navigate life in the big city."
That's a mistake. Start with a drive and then add your character traits to that. Dr. House wants to find out what's killing his
patient. That's his goal every single week. What makes him
compelling to watch are the character traits that are hung
onto that: he's brilliant but he hates people; he says horrible
things to the patients; he walks with a limp and is addicted
to Vicodin. If he had the character traits without the drive,
House would be just a jerk.

Now is this a firm and fast rule? Of course not. Fantastic writing can make a passive, goal-less character compelling. But
ask your students if they believe they are all fantastic writers.

For the ones who are truthful and say they're not, tell them that a character with drive who is active can overcome less-than fantastic writing. Take a look at the last *Bourne* movie. In my mind, not particularly well written or even well plotted. But you know what he wants (how did I become who I am?) and he is active in every single scene. You cannot deny it takes you on a ride (and got good reviews to boot).

Finally, I do think there should be some kernel of emotional truth in anything you're write. It's not always easy when your assignment is to write an episode of *Carpoolers,* but it should be your goal. Think of something you wouldn't tell anyone: not your spouse, maybe not even your therapist, and see if there is a way to make that a story, because trust me, it's something someone else has thought about.

That was what sparked me to write *Coma*. One day I thought, "How great would it be if I could be in a coma and live out my fantasies." And I've had literally, two dozen meetings with producers since then who said that script spoke to them in some way. I can't say that about anything else I've written. Oh, and I'm a big fan of short sentences. Short, declarative sentences.

Sometimes engaging more deeply with one's characters leads to the emergence of a natural plot, as Wendy explains.

 Wendy on Plot: "String Theory"

Plot is the thing I struggle most with in my own writing! I think that is because I often come up with themes first. I suppose I should be able to come up with a theme, and then think of a plot to illustrate it. But for me what works best is when I can come up with characters, then "let them go," watch what they do, and then deduce what the theme is from their actions (then go back and get rid of anything that is "in the way" of this). My best stuff has emerged when a scene just comes to me.

Scenes are plot points. If I see a scene in my mind, then I can get the characters and then I can see a string of things they will do … that "string of things" is the plot. One thing about plot, you can't make a character do something just because the plot needs that to happen. That's when you have people acting "out of character," which makes something seem fake. So I would say that if you can create good characters, they will make a plot happen.

Understanding the key elements of plot can help you to create one that you can really work with. Matt, who has worked in film for so many years, lays it out in terms that you can use.

Matt on Plot: "A Good Fight"

As for plot, my favorite definition of a story, and in its own way, plot, is this: Put your character in a tree. Throw rocks at him. Then get him down.

What I've learned is this:

Dramatic premise. That is a one-sentence description of the conflict of your novel. The dramatic premise of my latest novel is that weak people can become strong and triumph over overwhelming odds when they fight for something important. (This is different from the theme of the book, which is that good people will do bad things when their lives are on the line. The premise is more active than the theme and contains a seed of the conflict—good defeats evil. But the theme and premise go hand in hand.) My job now is to ensure that every action in the story supports and develops that premise. The plot has to back the premise up. And it has to do it in stages. If my heroine becomes strong in scene one, what's the point of the next 300 pages?

Some writers write from the outside in, they come up with an idea, develop a fully thought-out premise, outline their entire plot, and then write the novel. Some, like me, work from the inside out. I came up with a story idea, wrote an outline, which I more or less ignored once the novel got going, and then wrote the book. It wasn't until a few drafts in that I realized what my premise and theme were. Now I'm working to strengthen those.

Some smaller elements to keep in mind:

Rising action: The plot needs to be a series of escalations. Things have to keep getting worse for your character. The struggle has to get harder.

Goals: The character has a goal. The plot is composed of the obstacles put in his or her path on the way to reaching that goal.

Character growth: In my novel, the dramatic premise mirrors the character's growth as my heroine goes from a state of weakness to a state of strength. A character must change in the course of a story, and the plot is the mechanism that enacts that change.

For me, plot starts with conflict. Two characters have opposing goals. In my book, the heroine wants to live, the villain wants her dead. Simple. Make sure to give even attention to both. The villain must be as strong, crafty, and resourceful as the hero. You have to think about the plot from both sides of the coin, what each of the opposing characters wants. Don't let the hero, or one of the characters, win too easily. The opposing character has to put up a good fight. A good fight is what makes a story interesting.

What I so appreciate about Chris, Wendy, and Matt's philoso-
phies, which at times echo each other, and at times contradict, is
their absolute obsession with narrative, and their absolute dedi-
cation to the practice of writing. I've known them all since the
1980s, and their individual commitment to good storytelling
and the hard work that goes into it has never waned. Something
else that has never changed is their generosity in offering help
and feedback, and their openness to asking for feedback themselves (when their drafts are done).

Unfortunately, I can't pimp out my friends, but I can give you
some advice to help you find your own version of a Narrative
Brain Trust (NBT).

This advice is not so different from the dating advice that goes
something like, "If you are shopping for a purple ball gown, you
will find a purple ball gown." A Southern drag queen once told
me that. I hear she's looking for a Narrative Brain Trust to join.

Forming Your Own Narrative Brain Trust (NBT)

1. Look around. Who in your life already has a committed
   writing practice?

2. Who is truly obsessed with trying to understand the way
   stories work?

3. If you know someone who possesses the first two charac-
   teristics, for goodness sakes, snap him or her up and start
   sharing everything each of you knows about narrative, on
   a regular basis. Generously offer to read this person's work
   and give constructive feedback. And ask for the same in
   return.

4. If you don't, then go on the hunt. Join a writers' group (or form one), take a class, go to local reading series events, and remain actively alert for someone who meets criteria one and two, and then for God's sake take the advice in number three. Go! Now!

Some people are held together by their religious beliefs, others by politics or a particular cause. Let the love of narrative be the eternal bond that binds you to the members of your NBT. And when you are struggling through plot problems ask yourself, WWNBTD? Or just drop 'em a note and ask 'em.

Now that you are as obsessed with these matters as my friends and I are, perhaps you can keep going until you can't go no more! These exercises are meant to be done quickly; don't overthink them.

Exercise: Plot 'til You Plotz

Here are six tricks for mainlining narrative momentum.

1. Between the Numbers

Bullet out a list of ten plot points. Between two points drop in as many feasible obstacles for your protagonist as you can. Explore more during your writing hours, and include any of these new plot points that organically improve your narrative.

2. Index Cards

Write out all the actions that take place in your narrative on separate index cards. Shuffle them into a new random arrangement, and see if this new order gives you a new and energized view of your story.

3. Wanted

Write out the main "want" of each of your characters. Analyze how those wants conflict with each other. Where will all this conflict inevitably lead?

4. Trade Desires

Look at the wants from Step 3 and assign the same wants to different characters. Once again analyze how these wants conflict with each other, which will now be quite different. *Now* where will all this conflict inevitably lead?

5. Fight for the Right to Live

Pretend you are a real loathsome corporate honcho. One by one you are calling all of your employees (characters) in so that they can justify their places in the company. In the end you need to make a list of all employees, starting with Most Valuable at the top and working your way down. Then go through your story and see if the bottom employees can adapt and transform enough to keep their jobs, or else fire them!

6. Hire a Sub

Write one paragraph describing a potential subplot for your story. Then write half a page elaborating on how this subplot will complement your existing plot, and help move the narrative forward. Finally, try making your subplot your primary plot. Now what is your story?

Ultimately, there are some key points one must always keep in mind when constructing a strong plot. As usual, I have invented a zany mnemonic to match the material: P.L.O.T.W.I.C.H.

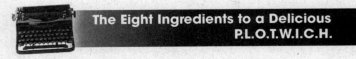

The Eight Ingredients to a Delicious P.L.O.T.W.I.C.H.

P = PREMISE

Weave an active premise throughout the story. "A liar destroys his intimate relationships through deception" is active. "Liars can't be intimate" is not.

L = LINKS

Link your scenes in a logical sequence. The logic does not have to be conventional; it *must,* however, be internally consistent.

O = OBSTACLES

Keep placing obstacles in your character's path.

T = TRANSFORMATION

Your character should grow, maybe even transform in a major way. This needs to happen one step at a time.

W = WANTS

Focus on what your character wants, in the big picture and in every scene.

I = IMPEDIMENTS

Impede your character's progress in getting what he wants. Delayed Gratification = Increased Suspense. Impediments = more obstacles that come quickly and toward the end.

C = CONFLICT

Put conflict in every scene.

H = HEAT

Turn the heat up gradually as the plot progresses, to build narrative momentum.

Memorize it, baby; but don't forget to season to taste. A recipe for a dish delish such as this is meant to be adapted and twisted by each individual artiste. Start plot-concocting and ready yourself to serve up a feast!

Finally, one important thing to bear in mind: how are you structuring your time?

Are you doing your hours?

If not, it's time to ask yourself:

- How do I need to restructure my day/week to support my writing needs?

- What/who in my life needs to end up on the cutting room floor, so that I can stay on track with my writing goal?

Think about it. Then take ACTION!

Kudos, Kiddo(s)!

You just learned (or revisited) a few strong perspectives on plot.

You have committed to developing your own NBT (Narrative Brain Trust).

You banged out a series of plot exercises.

You vowed to memorize the ingredients to a perfect PLOTWICH.

The Plot Thickens, Chickens! Pwok!

10

the play of writing

How does an actor know when the play has begun? The curtain rises, of course! When the show's over, the curtain falls. What does a dancer do before a performance? Warm up. Just like any other athlete must. Writing is both an exercise and a performance, so the rules of the actor and the athlete's game are the same for us. A little warmup goes a long way toward putting us in the mood to write and helping us to enter "the zone."

The Prelude

These days, when modern life is so filled with insidious interruptions, I think it is especially helpful to begin one's writing time with a cue, and end with one, too. When I run my Bang the Keys workshops, I usually sit in front of the clock and ask a workshopper to warn me when it's one minute before "showtime." Sometimes, when I'm feeling particularly divaesque, I demand that a gaggle of assistants powder-puff my face, spray my hair, and feed me a chewing-gum cigarette for effect. When the clock turns and the hour has begun, I light a candle. When the wick catches fire, we all know that the workshop evening has officially begun. When we are done, I blow out the candle. Over and out.

Arranging one's time is a huge part of this phase in one's writing practice. There is something about training your body and mind to begin and end an endeavor consciously, as in lighting a candle to start the workshop, blowing it out to end, that naturally carries over into the way you structure your writing life as a whole.

As always, focusing on a fun, doable micro (coming up with a writing "cue") can help with the much more intimidating macro (meeting your six-week writing goal, and ultimately finishing a large work).

Certainly a good way to prepare for one's writing hours is to try a meditation (as outlined in Chapter 6), or perhaps do a little quick journaling, but there are additional methods I'd recommend trying, just to change it up.

If you are aiming for 500 words a day, you can be as rigid as Graham Greene and literally end your writing day when you hit that lucky number. I would recommend, though, that once you are in a good writing jag you push yourself to write just a little more. Incrementally you may work up to 1,000 words a day or much more than that. But even if you stop at exactly 500 (or just under), good for you! That is a great way to end your writing day, by doing what you set out to do. The question, though, is how to *begin*?

Play the Cards

I enjoy pulling out a deck of cards at the beginning of my writing time, and putting them away when my hours are done. I've been reading tarot cards since I was a young gypsy. Before sitting down to write, I enjoy pulling a meditation card. Meditation, after all, is simply the act of focusing on one thing with relaxed concentration, and creating a boundary (or force-field, in my mind) to keep out all other things. The image and message of a card can sometimes help to close out the rest of the world, and help me tune in to my own creative world.

These days, I regularly play with what are called medicine cards. This deck, based on Native American mythology, contains pictures of 44 different animals. My friend Maureen first introduced me to this deck in 2001 and I've yet to become bored with them. The cards come with a wonderful book written by Jamie Sams and David Carson, who describe each animal as having its own special medicine or healing powers.

In my workshop, usually about halfway through the course, I pass the cards around so that each member can pick one. For the remainder of the workshop period that animal symbolizes the writer's secret super powers. For example, I am going to pull a card right now to symbolize the hidden super powers of all my workshoppers/coaching clients:

> Rrroarh! The Mountain Lion has appeared. Leadership! Sams and Carson note that this fierce cat serves as a reminder that it is a worthy endeavor to lead without demanding others to follow. I like this because as anyone who has ever read Shakespeare (or watched *Survivor* for that matter!) well knows: to lead often means to put oneself out there when no one else will, and perhaps risk being destroyed.

What a great symbol for the writer's life! All writers, pretty much, desire to finish their work and have it published or produced so that it exists in the "real world." Yet, a fear of what other people will think—of one's garbage draft, of one's never-perfect finished book or script—often inhibits writers from showing the courage to go forth without caring about public opinion.

I am certainly not immune to such things, but I have to say, whether it was nurture or nature, I was blessed to be born in this lifetime ... a complete eccentric. Yes, people, a kooky dame! As a child nothing gave me more pleasure than reveling in the charms of my imaginary world, and as I grew more socialized, finding others who were strong individuals and not afraid to twist to their own tune. As a child, my family gave me a great gift by always appreciating my creativity. My mother. My father. My sister. And for this I am eternally grateful.

When we were children, most of us had no problem connecting to the playful parts of our nature. If we wanted to sing we did, if we wanted to draw, we did. Then came middle school and beyond and all the pressures to be as boring and as bland as possible, all in an effort to fit in. I say, though, if you are compelled to write, you are compelled to play and to reengage with that uninhibited, kookadelic part of yourself. The trick is to be able to tap into it on command. That's where cues become key.

Be a mountain lion, not a cowardly lion, little lambs! And mix and match these rituals to begin and end your hours with. If you have to dress up in costume, so be it! Right now I am wearing a knock-off from *The Wiz*. It's a little itchy, but it is putting me in the mood.

Cues and Rituals: Top Ten

1. Cards. Shuffle and pull a card at the beginning of your writing time. Any symbolic deck will do: the animal cards, traditional tarot cards, I Ching cards, etc. Use this card to infuse your writing for the day. When your time is up, put your cards away. Observe tradition and wrap them nicely in a silk cloth.

2. Music. Improvise on an instrument or play a song on your stereo or your headphones. Recently, when I started playing piano, I felt compelled to improvise, to express my feelings so that I could hear them. Perhaps you can bring a harmonica to your writing space and play the blues. Or pick a song at random on your computer, play it on your headphones, and let that music set the tone for the next couple of writing hours.

3. Dictionary. Choose a word at random from the dictionary and begin your day's writing by using that word. Or simply write the word out and keep it in mind during your day's work. When you are done, write a sentence using that word, and connecting it (even in a wild, illogical way) to your story. Use your PC—Project Cahier—to keep a record of these sentences.

4. Read Your IC. In your Inner Cahier, you will find plenty of raw emotional material to put you in the mood to write. Read a section at random and then try to channel those particular emotions into your day's writing. End by writing a journal entry about how it felt.

5. Move. Do a little stretching or yoga. Or put on a pair of 1970s gym shorts and tube socks and do some jumping jacks. Or do the H-Dance, the Happy Dance invented by my college roommate Debbie Taylor and me (actually we ripped off Snoopy from the Peanuts cartoons). We often

danced the Happy Dance to summon up some enthusiasm and eventually our other roommates, Rachel and Maura, followed suit; so beware, unless you are in a private place, you may inadvertently form a conga line. Create your movement to end your workday by.

6. Sentence-Piration. Choose a sentence at random from any book and use it as a jumping-off point for your day's writing. Choose another sentence at random, purely to meditate on, when the day is done. Make a few notes about what the ending sentence made you think of; you may want to use this in your next writing session.

7. Act Out. Get into character by reading your previous day's work aloud, and make an attempt to really "perform" the roles of the different characters. Perhaps get up and walk around as your character, put on a costume piece—special shoes or eyeglasses—or maybe just tuck in your shirt the way he would, to begin your performance "from the outside in."

8. Pep Talk. Be like Ali and tell yourself you are The Greatest. But don't be generic. Validate what you really appreciate about yourself as a writer. At the end, write down all that you did well. (Kudos, people, kudos!)

9. MC Hammer. Imagine you are being filmed for a documentary about writers, or you about to give a speech or a reading. Pretend you are the emcee and introduce yourself to the audience. At the end, sign off in some writerly way.

10. Play a Writing Game. Pick any from this book or make up your own to begin your session with. At the end, write down what the "takeaway" was for you.

Minimize the Distractions

Before we cut to Kudos and close out this chapter, I need to warn you about something absolutely terrible. Oh wait, someone just added me on Facebook, I'll fill you in later. All right! All right! I'll tell you … here it is: all of the above exercises, and my little "be yourself, you kook" pep talk were meant to show you how to carve out writing time that has a clear beginning and clear end, just like a class you take or teach, or a job you clock in and clock out of. But what of all the little distractions of the universe, from your own beloved family, to your day-job homework, and of course the ever-present pull of the Internet and other techno-crack?

If I could come in there and pick up your phone when it rings and tell your slacker pal Charlie, "Dude, he can't have lunch with you, he's working. Call back at three," I would. (You'd think Charlie Rose would be busier, but the guy likes to chat and chew!) The fact is, you need to work consciously each day to create and maintain that force-field around your writing time. The rituals help, because they make your practice more professional, with a beginning and an end, like a job. They suggest that no, you cannot do mindless "research" on how many times snoods were worn in noir films of the '40s, or the dietary habits of the star-nosed mole.

And although I encourage you to channel the playful young child in you, I highly discourage you from allowing your inner mean teen to intrude with lame excuses such as: "But I'll just stay online while I'm working, in case one of my buddies really needs me," or "I'll work on this other stuff first."

There's no easy answer. You will have your good days and your bad days, but each day that you have writing hours scheduled, you should try your hardest to insulate yourself from the mob and the mania of mindless channel-surfing. Go back to *my* style of channel-surfing instead: meditation.

I was recently told that one of my favorite authors, Paul Auster, does not "do e-mail." You want to contact him, you fax him. Very old world! My childhood pal Susan is very old world, too, and not one for the banal shortcuts of modern life. She prefers live conversation over e-mail quickies, and sitting down for a meal rather than eating on the go. Sometimes quality and plea-sure take more time. And always, they are worth it. If you do your quality writing work, and play your heart out, treat your-self to a fun hang with a friend or a pleasant meal afterward. Perhaps for those six hours a week (minimum) when you are doing your job of writing your project (your official project, dears, not 20 new ones) you can be out of touch so that you can stay in touch with yourself, your words, maybe even your life's work. That's the fax, Jack!

Kudos, Kiddos!

You came up with your own cue/ritual for your writing time.

You are making a conscious effort to maintain your writing force-field.

Without being all contrived about it, you have already sum-moned up some of your super powers.

step 3

nurture

Nurture your project with love so others may love it, too.

11

the fishbowl

You did it, baby! You began with your strongest idea; you are arranging your material into a concrete structure; now, you are ready to nurture your project with love, so that others may love it, too. This section is all about loving your baby. Let's begin this part of the adventure by going back in time, to a simpler, more heartfelt era, shall we? Yes, dears: the '80s!

Behind the Fishbowl

When I was in college, I worked for a few semesters as a counselor and then a director, at The Hear-to-Help-Hotline (get it, *Hear*-to-Help), the campus crisis intervention service. The Hotline (and walk-in service) had been created a few years earlier by students at our school, the State University of New York at Purchase, in response to a suicide on campus.

The skills I learned here served as a foundation for pretty much all of the challenges I would later face, personally and professionally, as a human being on this planet: active listening; staying calm but connected during a crisis (still workin' on that one, Toots); making my hotline beeper go off and pretending I had to respond to an urgent call because I needed to escape a tedious conversation. Actually, I still use that old trick almost daily!

Forgive the gallows humor. Believe me, I have dealt with suicide in my own life, and I have counseled many suicidal people, during college and during my years on the phone at the New York City Department of Health AIDS Hotline. It was while doing hotline counseling I learned this: a little humor goes a long way to release tension when you have to face potential tragedy day after day. Counseling people (always anonymously) during their times of great fear and despair also gave me some perspective about writing. The writing process is often joyous and tremendously satisfying; at other times it is frustrating and faith-testing. But it is not life and death (despite most writers' penchant for drama).

Yet from real life we can certainly transfer a lot of skills into our writing practice. Ain't that a kick in the head?!

Although dealing with a potential suicide on our campus hotline was actually rare, it was of course the situation that every newbie counselor most feared. At the culmination of our intensive training weekend we participated in a group counseling exercise, called the Fishbowl. Sounds nautical, and even naughty, doesn't it? Well, not exactly, but this experience did stay with me and inspire a writing exercise that is always a workshop favorite.

Picture the scene: a group of altruistic 19- and 20-year-olds, circa the late 1980s, sitting in a circle, the girls with high hair, the guys with spiky 'dos. Many with arms entwined. Some resting their feet on piles of hacky-sack cushions. It was a somber, yet touchy-feely, crunchy granola scene. Did Tracy Chapman provide the soundtrack or the Smiths? I can't recall. But I digress!

The hotline director sat in the middle of a circle and played the role of a suicidal caller. A volunteer counselor-in-training played the primary counselor on duty and would sit back to back with the "caller" (the idea being, when you are on the phone you cannot read body language—or notice the garishness of '80s fashion, I suppose). The Primary Counselor began the dialogue, and after a few minutes the rest of us were directed to provide some back up. One person would throw a question out to the caller, and then others would chime in.

It was as if all of us sitting in the circle were one counselor, trained in the art of asking open-ended questions designed to get the caller talking and revealing himself, each in an effort to form a real connection with this person, a connection that could be the difference between life and death. I must add, of course, as anyone who has dealt with suicide in real life, or has done this kind of work, surely knows: if someone is intent on killing himself, there is absolutely nothing anyone else can do to stop him. The ones who call a hotline are more likely to be "saved," because they are reaching out for help.

Jump into the Bowl

When I began teaching writing workshops, I had a feeling that this "fishbowl" technique could be incredibly helpful if used to produce a series of questions about a character-in-progress. If a character is close to creative death—meaning you really don't understand how to get her to open up; you've lost or perhaps never had the ability to communicate with her, to understand her life, who she really is—then you need to apply urgent measures, right? The nice thing about this game is that it is *not* about actual life and death, thank goodness; it's just a great way to learn more about one of the people you are spending so much time with (your character), and when played with a group of co-conspirators (like the writing buddies you're sharing this book with) it can be a blast, and quite illuminating, even if you feel like you know your character completely.

This game has often been of great help to my workshoppers who are on a third or fourth draft of their stories. It's as if they've gotten so close to the people in their stories and plays that they can't see them anymore. This happens in real life, too, so don't feel bad. The point is to stop brooding and start connecting. Or keep brooding and start connecting. Dealer's choice.

To illustrate, allow me to give you a quick character sketch.

Sample Fishbowl

He's a youngish married man with a wife and two kids. The story takes place in the 1950s. He used to live in Greenwich Village with his wife and believed they were destined for some kind of greatness. He ended up in a Connecticut suburb working a soul-numbing, white-collar business job. He and his wife still dream of chucking it all and moving to Paris to live like Bohemians. But fear, infidelity, alcohol, and unexpected pregnancy all seem to get in the way of them taking this great leap.

What questions come to mind?

Here's a sampling that could be evoked from the paragraph above, and I'm sure you can think of many, many more. As you will see, the questions need not all connect directly to the brief sketch.

What's his name and what does he look like?

What kind of music does he listen to?

Who was his first love?

How do men respond to him when he enters a room? Women?

What does he love most about each of his children? What does he secretly or unconsciously dislike, even hate, about them?

What does his laugh sound like?

Does he play any sports? Which ones?

How is his wife different from (or similar to) his past girlfriends?

How does his father treat his mother?

What is his greatest regret, and what is his proudest moment?

The character described in this sample is Frank Wheeler, the protagonist of Richard Yates's great novel, *Revolutionary Road*. A little side note on Yates, very much a "writer's writer." For years, Yates felt tortured by the ups and downs of the publishing world's fickle response to him. In particular, he suffered over *The New Yorker*'s continual rejection of his short stories. Years later, the iconic magazine published a Yates story posthumously. I asked a friend who knew a staff editor from that era if she could find out why they rejected his stories during his life. She nosed around and received this succinct reply: "I guess we didn't like them."

If a writer as great and admired as Yates was subject to such random reactions, it should offer some reassurance! And this was a fellow who did his work—dedicated himself to his craft, his characters. Nevertheless, most every serious writer has to suffer through rejection and come to terms with the nature of the business; every writer must also reconcile himself with the fact that he is going to have to write much, much more than will actually end up in his finished work.

Patricia Highsmith said she had to throw out the first 70 or more pages of *The Talented Mr. Ripley* after she discovered she was writing prose that was too slack, not taut and nervous enough to fit the main character's personality. Throwing out pages is part of the process. Just make sure to save the "bad" material; seeds of something sublime could be hidden in the garbage.

After a work is completed, though, I've never heard any writer speak of regretting his forays down those blind alleys, or making those excursions into terrain that provided only back-story and character insights, but which never ended up in the final version. So remind yourself: you may fill pages with character questions and answers and end up only using 10 percent—or less—of what you discover.

I read a recent essay by Malcolm Gladwell called "Late Bloomers" that described the process by which late-blooming artists approach their craft, compared to young prodigies. Essentially, it takes many writers and artists years of practice to reach their peak performance level. Gladwell used the example of Ben Fountain, who achieved literary fame in his late 40s. In the piece, Fountain gave heartfelt thanks to his wife, who never questioned his process, his talent. Gladwell compared Fountain's wife, Sharon, to what, in other eras, might have been called a "patron." All writers who must make a living in this world need patrons. *Emotional* patrons. And if you are not lucky enough to have one or many, I say try *being* one, and watch the patronage as it is returned tenfold.

And if it takes a village to raise a child, then it certainly could only help to enlist the aid of your writing pals, friends, bartenders, and other allies to form and fully nurture your characters into an evolved form. If you can trying this exercise with your writing group would be ideal, but it is not essential. Get going, Goldie.

Exercise: The Fishbowl

1. Each writer presents a quick sketch of one character who he or she is trying to get to know better. If there's anything significant about the context of the story, please share as necessary.

2. The other members of the group will shoot out questions for the author. This can be done "fishbowl" style, meaning there's no need to go around in a circle or be overly formal. Just try not to talk over each other, and give the writer enough time to jot down the questions. The writer is not supposed to respond with answers. He will do that later, during his writing time. The writer in the "hot seat" should get about 10 minutes to receive questions. The next person up should receive the same amount of time, and so on. Manners, darling!

3. For homework, the writer should answer all of these questions as fully as possible. If other questions arise, answer those, too. If certain ones are real head-scratchers, make

up something. If truly stumped, though, just highlight those questions to answer later; don't use a difficult question as an excuse to stop writing. Instead: move on … dot org!

This exercise is especially helpful when you are facing a blank page, feeling tired or uninspired. Simply answer the questions with as much energy, curiosity, and compassion as possible, and you will probably fill up at least a few pages, maybe even 10, maybe more. This exercise can be used again and again for all the different characters in your piece. You can also use it to elicit story questions by focusing on plot instead of character. See what your audience is curious about in terms of action, setting, and general construction of the narrative.

Fishing Alone

If you do not have a writer's group, then form one, and use this book as your syllabus. If that's not possible, perhaps you have a book club (or can create or join one). See if you can get 10 minutes of time on your club's dime to do the above exercise. If you are not in any kind of group, try e-mailing a bunch of your friends, or finding just one playful pal who will indulge you. (These days most people are eager to be distracted at work by random e-mails from their friends; you shouldn't have a hard time finding takers.)

Another option is to post a basic character sketch on whatever social networking sites you belong to, and ask those buddies to provide questions for you. With this method, I suspect you'll get enough questions to develop a character who becomes a true friend to you, even if this friend is a fictional murderer or psychopath. Judge not!

If you can't find anyone (which to be honest, I find hard to swallow—even in prison, I have a feeling one sympathetic guard and a bored inmate with nothing to do but sharpen his shank will be willing to help), there's still hope. Simply use the 20-plus questions provided in this chapter. You'll find your way.

The great thing about this little game is that it will give you a strong, early sense of what your potential readers (or audience members, if you are writing a play or screenplay) already connect to in your story's characters.

And it's a remarkable fact that other people can come up with a nearly endless variety of wonderful nosy questions about your creation, if you make it into a game for them (what a nice rehearsal for what you will be doing for your readers). Conversely, I am certain it will feel much easier for you, at first, to bang out a dozen questions about someone else's cowboy novella, and the inner and outer life of a rancher on the range named Pierre, even if you are 100 percent city mouse, born and raised, and you detest westerns (and French-Canadian cowboys to boot!) with a passion.

It's just magically easier to be generous with someone else's tale and players, whereas for your own story you may lose patience and energy; you may feel too much pressure; you may just have days, or weeks, or months when (for unconscious reasons we'll explore later in this section) you simply feel too lost, resentful, incompetent, scared, angry (you fill in the tortured writer adjective here) to explore your own creation. And if you are writing a memoir, forget it. You will surely have dark, anxious moments when you are too influenced by your real-life relationships to your characters (and your fear of what your relatives and friends will say when the book comes out) to be as objective and creative as you need to be. But by getting into this playful mode for other writers, you will soon learn how to be just as loose yet probing with your own work.

Hook Your Reader

Remember the initial "Bang" in "Bang the Keys"—inspired by four Hebrew letters, Yud Hei Vav Hei? The "Vav" translates literally from Hebrew to the English word "hook," as in what hooks a reader? This experience can be just like a first date full of many questions, from the informational (Where do you live? Where'd you grow up? Where'd your parents grow up?) to the emotional (How did you feel when your sister the atheist suddenly became born-again?) to the whimsical as well as totally out of left field (If you could be any type of animal what would you be? If you knew someone who wanted to marry their car would you attend the ceremony, and what would you bring as a gift?).

You may discover that you don't have enough chemistry to connect to your own character. And if that's the case, so what? Develop another. If you keep having this experience, though, you should seriously stop complaining about all of them and ask yourself what your resistance is. But I'm an optimist, and I hope that this game will be a first step in finding and keeping a character you feel passion for and connection to.

Who knows what will ultimately "hook" your reader in the finished rendition of this character? Whatever it is, it is surely not going to be a single answer to a random question. Just like in real life, we connect to people because of a combination of intangibles. We stay connected because we keep in touch, and dare I say, keep it real?

Using this exercise as a form of communication with your characters is an effective way to develop and hone a richer relationship with them. If you are in the revision stage of your writing process, this could be especially helpful. You may have convinced yourself that you know everything there is to know about your characters. Even as you read this, you may already be cracking and admitting that you don't know as much about your people as you should!

This game is often doubly helpful for writers who are creating characters on the page who also exist or existed in real life. Perhaps those people are the family members featured in your essay or memoir, or the historical figures you are weaving into your short story or novel. It's natural for writers to feel as if they already know these people inside and out. And yet they also realize they are missing something about these folks, something that other people might be able to help them see more clearly.

In some of my Bang the Keys workshops, the following questions have been asked. And these are just a sampling, a tasting plate, if you will. Be warned: I do tend to encourage a certain percentage of randy questions. It just keeps the evening lively!

- What part of her body does she think is the sexiest? The least sexy?

- What's the most awful thing she's ever said to anyone?

- What's a physical habit she unconsciously exhibits on a regular basis?

- Are her grandparents alive? What are her relationships with them?

- If she were a song, what song does she think she'd be? What song would her worst enemy think she is?

- In her view, what's her signature "hot" sexual move? What do her lovers think? If she were videotaped making that move, would she laugh or run screaming from the room? What would Larry King say?

- How does she deal with confrontation?

- Who is she most envious of and why?

- What's the outfit she's worn that she is most embarrassed by still?

- Does she drink coffee in the morning? Or tea? Nothing? What's her start-of-the-day ritual?

- What is she like as a traveler? How rigid/flexible/adventurous is she?

- What's the most perverse sexual experience she's ever had? And can you give me the number of the person she had it with?

- What food does she crave but avoid? Why?

- Is she more likely to play air guitar or sing into her hairbrush when a great '80s record comes on, and what song makes her jump out of her bar seat and yell, "This is MY SONG!"

In addition to greedily devouring questions for your own piece of work, you should also dip into any compelling inquiries that come up for your co-conspirators during this game. You can use the questions that arise for other people's characters: How many siblings does he have? How does he feel about animals? What's his secret talent? Boxers or briefs? That last one has been asked, without fail, in every workshop I've ever led! Thanks, Bill Clinton.

Pretty soon you won't need the outside prompts. You'll be able to come up with a slew of varied questions on your own. It's usually best, though, to write out those questions when you are not sitting down for your official writing time. If you are doing this exercise solo, give yourself a 10 minute, 20 question limit, and play the game when you need to just kill time: riding the train, waiting in the dentist's office, avoiding a boring task at your day job.

Still, this game is definitely best played with a group. Ultimately you are aiming to complete and share your work with others. What a reader or viewer brings to a story is at once unique and universal, because we are all human. Think of the fishbowl as a foreshadowing of the communion your audience will experience with your story. Leave space for surprise and spontaneity, and take every question as an opportunity to get to know your characters a little better. Because your creations stem from inside you, be prepared for them to play a key role in helping you to understand yourself better, too. Any questions?

Kudos, Kiddo(s)!

You engaged with your characters on a much deeper level.

You enlisted the help of others, and provided help in return.

You gained plenty of questions to riff off of, and do not have to worry about facing the blank page.

12

the unconscious: *uncensored!*

Writing isn't something you do in a vacuum. Even if you are lucky enough to find a room of your own to do your hours in, you still have to leave it every day, to engage with loved ones, day jobs, and whatever else.

After a couple of weeks of good, honest work on your project you may find that you feel resentful of friends whom you start to see as walking distractathons to your newfound writer's life. You may begin to admit to yourself that certain relationships are what I call bore-tox (no relation to Botox or Gore-Tex). No, these are relationships that self-help books would describe as toxic (and rightly so) because at best they pull you away from the writer's life you are developing, and at worst are blatantly destructive. Bad enough, yes? But the reason I don't just call these relationships merely toxic is their other element: *they are boring.*

These are the involvements with friends and relatives who are adept at always shifting the focus of the conversation back to them. Usually they are bored and unhappy and need to just blather on about the same boring problems they've had for years, and yet when you suggest constructive actions they can take, they always find a way to shoot down your ideas. They are what my college teacher who oversaw our Hotline called "help-rejecting complainers." No matter what you suggest to these permanently unhappy types, they give you a reason why they can't do this, can't do that, are simply "unlucky." Exactly what you are trying *not* to be, by actually making constructive changes in your life. Perhaps these are people who are always immersed in one kind of crazy drama or another.

Maybe there's an alcohol or drug issue, or untreated depression, or maybe these are folks who have been abused and mistreated during much of their lives, and can't seem to dig themselves out of the cycle, can't seem to ask for help, or accept it when it's offered. Maybe they are just poor listeners. Often they will be jealous of the fact that you are pulling yourself out of a dead period in your life.

Don't Get Sucked into the Bore-tox!

With some of these folks, it may be time to stop returning those phone calls, and let the relationships drift until they barely exist. Where family is concerned, you may just have to set very firm boundaries about your writing time, and how much limited head-space you now have with which to play therapist/parent. Maybe you can connect a couple of these bores? Just put a mirror in each set of hands and point them toward each other.

The point is, you know that change is imminent and urgently needed, but your conscious mind is probably telling you "Well, next time I'll say something" or "She's not so bad." (Your unconscious mind, however, will not be fooled. It knows that your writing, which is an extension of you, and your very life force, is worth protecting and that you deserve the respect of being left alone to do your work.)

Dream-Weaving

One way the unconscious communicates is through dreams. If you view your dream life as a friend, an Obi-Wan Kenobi–style ally who is ready to share its wisdom with you any time you are willing to receive, you are already way ahead of the game. You are likely to gradually become the lucky recipient of helpful direction on how to navigate your waking life (relationships, work, money, etc.) in such a way that your writing life is well-supported. And from these nighttime adventures, you are also likely to receive helpful ideas for your actual writing practice. Pretty cush, darling!

And now more than ever, during these overstimulated, information-saturated times, we can all use as much help as we can get with tuning in to our intuition, and tuning out the white noise. (If you are Googling "how to meditate" right now, that pretty much illustrates the paradox!)

Swiss psychoanalyst Carl G. Jung believed that it was necessary to understand the meaning of a dream "sign," a specific symbol, in the mind of the dreamer. For instance, a black cat might mean bad luck to one person, mystery to another, and an allergy attack to the next. No dream is static in its meaning, just as no dream symbol is. The person with bad allergies who dreams of a black cat on Tuesday and associates it with sneezing and suffering might dream of a black cat on Wednesday and associate it with dominatrices and delight.

Although Jung himself was a pioneer in his study of archetypes, and the collective unconscious, and symbols that we as humans may all relate to, he was not a literalist. He worked to make clear that each person has his own psyche and his own dream language. And each person's dreams may contain messages, fantasies, "forgotten" memories, and psychic visions.

Philip K. Dick saw visions (waking and sleeping) that fed into his dream life as well as his waking life. He integrated many of those visions into his fiction.

Graphic novelist Art Spiegelman, best known for his *Maus* books, has worked a great deal with his unconscious night world. In fact, he wrote several comic strips that he titled "Real Dreams," based on actual dreams.

Poet Maya Angelou has compared dreams to what in West Africa is called "deep talk"—parables or axioms shared by wise elders.

Go Off Duty for the Night

There's a method I recommend for working with dreams that's quite effective, and basically follows a Jungian model. (As always, though, feel free to experiment as you wish and adapt this exercise in whatever way works for you.) First, buy a separate journal just for your dreams. (Yes, I have a scam I'm running with the stationery stores. Every time one of you suckers buys a journal I get a buck. Wait a second, in this economy maybe I should ask myself: who's the sucker? I'm calling Moe at

Acme Stationery right now and demanding a bigger piece of the pie!) Anyway ... keep this journal by your bed with the intention of writing down your dreams in the morning.

You may already be exclaiming, "But I never remember my dreams!!" Relax, doll, and pace yourself. This is a gradual process, and it's perfectly normal to not remember much in the first week or two. But trust in the process, and in true Bang the Keys style, just keep it up, keep practicing.

I suggest silently repeating this message to yourself, as you are getting ready to sleep: "I am going off duty now. Unconscious: you take over." You can also pose a question about your writing to your unconscious, and you may just wake up with the answer or a fresh idea.

If you wish, tell yourself your intention is to remember your dreams in the morning. It may work for some of you right away. If you are the type of person who can tell yourself to wake up at a certain time—like when you have to catch a plane in the morning—and you find yourself rising a minute before your alarm goes off, you'll probably see quick results. But if you need more time to train your mind, do not worry a bit. Simply by doing this exercise regularly, you are placing yourself on the tarmac. This method is much more reliable than taking the Van Wyck Expressway to JFK, any day of the week!

Work With Your Dreams

Think of your unconscious as a trusted friend with whom you are taking a fascinating road trip. You are going to see many sights on this journey: some exciting, some sexy, some scary, and some downright strange. But it's a long trip and you have worked hard all day and are very tired. Give your good friend the keys to the car; you sleep while your buddy drives.

This little meditative image is especially helpful if you regularly have trouble sleeping, or find yourself lying awake in bed at night worrying about all the anxiety-provoking aspects of your daily life. Forget about the dream exercise for a second, this sleep-inducing, fear-and-self-loathing reducing practice could save you all that money you would've spent on Ambien or old-fashioned whiskey! And by the way, do not try working with your dreams when you are under the influence of any mind-altering substance, or too much rich food. You may find it's like trying to play an out-of-tune instrument, or attempting to run several miles without warming up. Best to work with dreams when your body is in a healthy state.

Let's say you had a dream in which your Aunt Louise was sitting on a giant turtle in the desert, drinking a cup of coffee. Write out the details just like that, but in parentheses after every person, place, or thing, note your first, uncensored association. Example: Aunt Louise (battle ax). If you have three different dreams about Aunt Louise, you may have three different associations: battle ax, living saint, and retro nympho, for instance. The unconscious is rarely linear and logical. So let's take a look at how this would play out:

My Aunt Louise (battle ax) was sitting atop a giant turtle (cute monster) in the desert (lonely place) drinking a cup of coffee (something ordinary).

Now read the sentence back to yourself replacing the initial objects with the associations. Remember those Mad-Libs notebooks, when you were a kid? Or Match Game, the "fill in the blanks" TV show with such fab and saucy players as Charles

Nelson Reilly and Brett Somers? ("I need to make *blank* at
my job before I can feel rich." Hint, the answer was often
"whoopee.") It's the same idea. You may have to make a little
tweak or two to unmask a somewhat coherent story, but that
shouldn't be too hard. And if there was any identity-shifting
going on in the dream—perhaps the woman on the turtle
looked like Aunt Louise but it felt like she was actually you—
make note.

So ultimately you would read the sentence back like this:
A battle ax, possibly me (!), sat atop a cute monster taking in
something ordinary.

Maybe the next part involves Louise (really you, let's assume)
screaming for help. As you write out the whole story, with your
instant associations, not the strange, literal things like giant
turtles and deserts, you are bound to see a story emerge. After
reading the new version of your dream through once, the next
step is to ask yourself what you think the dream means. Put your
answer into one concise sentence, two if absolutely necessary.
Keep it simple. The most important element of this exercise
is this: *Do Not Censor Yourself.* The unconscious is here to help
you to deal with things that are too threatening for your conscious mind to look at during the day. It's natural, then, for some
pretty disturbing things to come up at night.

I stopped the dream here, but I suspect it could have gone one
or two ways. Perhaps Aunt Louise, or you, rather, called for help
and received the aid that you needed. That could have been a
happy-ending sort of dream, and afterward maybe you'd make
a connection between a monster of a problem in your ordinary
life for which you really should ask for help ... because by asking you are likely to receive. Or maybe you hollered for help

desperately and no one came. What then? You may have to accept the fact that you're on your own. Maybe you are in some sort of a terrible situation (that from the outside appears ordinary) for which you cannot get outside help, you have to help yourself. Not a pleasant thought, I know. But the thing about the unconscious is that it is completely honest, and will share its wisdom with you because it believes you need to be more aware. And besides, the unconscious isn't some nosy neighbor or hall monitor butting into your business—it's you, babe!

The unconscious is an amorphous subject. Following is a concrete way to deal with your slippy and surreal subcon'.

Exercise: Dream Journaling

1. Keep your dream journal by your bedside, and before going to sleep tell yourself, "I'm off duty; unconscious— take over." Also, focus your mind for a moment on your intention to remember your dreams in the morning. Pose a specific question to your unconscious if you wish.

2. When you first wake up (before you have a chance to forget): write down each dream you can recall, in narrative form. Next to every person, place, or thing, in parentheses, write your first association with that object. Limit yourself to a word or phrase, and don't feel as if you need to stay with that association every time. Do not censor yourself!

3. Now read over what you wrote, this time ignoring the literal people, places, and things, and instead substituting your associations.

4. Write down in one sentence what you think the message of your dream is. Be honest. No one will read this but you.

5. If you can't remember your dream clearly, yet still wake up with an answer or idea in your mind related to your writing, note it in detail.

6. Try to maintain this practice consistently, and pay attention to patterns that start to emerge.

Get the Message

For writers, the unconscious can feel like a blessing and a curse. As noted above, when you work with your dreams, you may start to notice a pattern to the messages. If after a few months you see that you consistently have dreams in which you are being crushed by debts, perhaps it's time to write a big check to Visa, and then cut up your charge plates. (When did that phrase go out of fashion? It's so yummy!)

You are also very likely to receive some truly helpful input around your writing. The input could be practical, such as a reminder that you write better in the morning than at night. This nudge could push you to plan on getting up early most days to work on your novel, rather than waiting till 9 P.M. when you're exhausted. Or you could receive intuitive advice about a plot point that has been frustrating you, or the tone of the whole book—what about trying your epic family saga, *The Nut Jobs*, as a comedy not a tragedy? Just sayin'. There could be a supporting player in your novel who actually needs a much meatier character arc. You might as well experiment, because the unconscious really does have your best interests at heart. It is not an annoying distraction, or self-absorbed bore-tox; it's that friend who drove all night while you slept. So treat it with some respect.

However, it may ask you to look at some aspects of your life that you may not feel ready to deal with. What if it's about your marriage of 10 years? The new job you moved halfway across the country for? What if your unconscious keeps gently pushing you to look at problems in these areas? You may panic, as I have, and feel anxiety about having to do something. In meditative terms, though, all you really need to do is observe your feelings in the moment, note your observations. Still, opening up the Pandora's Box of your unconscious could give you the willies. It has certainly given me the Jillies! And trust me, I do scare easily.

Everyday folks don't have to worry as much about this sort of thing. And when you are not leading a writing life, you don't have to either. But let's be honest, as you begin to commit more to your writing practice, and move more deeply into the content of your work, you are connecting more to yourself, and opening up that door of the unknown anyway.

If you don't want to use your powers of introspection, don't be a writer; simply commit to being a floozy and have some fun while you can, missy! But if you are compelled to write, you must grapple with yourself. You know that, of course. And your unconscious is just here to remind you, just like I am.

As you write, anyway, you are probably starting to deal with your emotions around many of the key aspects of your life. I've had numerous private writing clients who have reached a point in their work where they are really starting to find their voice, nail their story, hone their craft, and usually right around that turning point time, there is a great panic. I've seen countless clients write about relationships, marriages, affairs … and worry that their partners and other loved ones will read what they write and hate them.

I try to explain that oftentimes working through your conflicts on the page can actually help to blow off some steam that would just play out as nagging and carping on the home front. I reassure them that they need to allow themselves to write from bits of pieces of real life, and the real characters in their lives if need be, so long as they promise (in front of a priest, a notary, and a hit man) that they will only paint their dear writing coach in the most favorable light. (Amazing how she came from such humble beginnings and emerged as such an inspirational heroine; so eternal, so funny, so sexy. And beautiful Maura Tierney, if you are reading this, I give you the green light to play me in *Sage-Coach*, a Lifetime Moment of Truth movie.)

My TV-movie fantasies aside, there is one more important aspect of your unconscious I want to leave you with.

Face Your Anxiety

A few years ago I was out for brunch with my friend Clarinda. Clarinda is an all-around artist. Her mom is Iris Lezak, the abstract expressionist painter, who provided my workshoppers with such helpful insight on discipline and daily practice; her Dad was Jackson Mac Low, the pioneering "chance" poet. Clarinda dances, choreographs, directs, writes, and is well known in the New York performing arts scene. Her business card reads "catalyst". And thank goodness for me, that's exactly what she is.

As we sat in HK (a restaurant in Hell's Kitchen—get it?), I told her about this bit of bum luck: I'd torn my ACL playing tennis. The only way to repair this main ligament in the knee, I'd been advised, was surgery.

This was February; I'd had the accident the previous August and within a day was fine, sort of. But my balance had been off for months, and my leg did feel a little wobbly; it was hard to run … even like a girl. Still, when I saw a sports medicine doctor I expected him to recommend physical therapy, not an operation. This news threw me into a cyclone of worries.

I was teaching at New York University, teaching and working toward my MFA at the New School, and seeing clients. Dear Clarinda listened as I thought out loud about the main source of my anxiety: when to schedule my surgery with my complicated and tight schedule.

Clarinda said that she knew a lot of dancers who had this very same surgery and made a suggestion: "Why don't you do the surgery in August, when you have a whole month off from school?" The moment she said that I felt my body relax, and my mind calm down. She was completely right, and I knew it. Arranging that time and space to heal and recover at my own pace, at a time when I did not have to leave my house to teach, seemed like a brilliant idea. Why didn't I think of it?!

That night, I was riding the E train downtown to meet my friends Wendy and Joe for a movie. I felt more relaxed than I had since my surgeon broke the news about my busted knee. As the train rumbled downtown I thought about my writing (which I'd unknowingly set on auto-pilot). I was working on small non-fiction pieces for my New School degree. Everything I wrote was good. Fine. Garnered a positive response. But it wasn't going to change anyone's life, and even I didn't feel so inspired by what I was doing. My writing had no passion, no humor.

I closed my eyes and held my notebook and pen steady on my lap. I asked my unconscious a question: What do I really want to write? The answer came to me immediately: the movies. Why hadn't I thought of that before? I had dipped into the movies here and there, but hadn't made it my focus, even though it was such a great love, and such a key element of my New York City childhood. That next week I had an angle for my thesis. The next month one of my essays, about my father and the movies, was accepted for publication in *New York Stories*, one of my favorite magazines.

The realization I had on that train ride helped me immediately, and has helped me with every writing project since, plus it is a truth that I have since passed on to countless clients:

> Anxiety creates a barrier between a writer and her creativity. *Remove the anxiety, the creativity flows.*

I was lucky to have a catalyst pal like Clarinda give me the initial jolt, but the "takeaway" I leave you with is this: when you are feeling stuck in rote, disconnected writing, do your dream work, and be patient while the internal cleaning mechanism slowly clicks into gear, but when in doubt, ask yourself "what am I most anxious about?" And ask your unconscious for some help with a solution.

When you start taking the advice of your unconscious, you will then have the wherewithal to ask yourself this key question: *What do I* want *to write?*

Listen to the response that immediately pops into your mind. Don't censor yourself!!

And as always, maintain your sense of humor and sense of play. After all, sometimes a giant turtle is just a giant turtle. Then again, sometimes a ball buster is all that and more ... buster!

Kudos Kiddo(s)!

You engaged with difficult blocks to your writing life.

You opened the door to dealing with dreams.

You took a step toward removing anxiety, and opening up to creativity.

I'm spent! Time for a nap.

13

sex, money, and one magic word

My sideline for many years has been as an astrologer. Although I've written quick and dirty 'scopes for mags, my real interest in the craft is much more esoteric, even eggheady. Carl Jung wrote at length about the subject, and studied it seriously, as did lauded writers Italo Calvino and Jorge Luis Borges, as well as French philosopher, composer, and humanist astrologer Dane Rudhyar who called the craft "The Algebra of Life."

My fascination with the esoteric, deeper level of stargazing is connected to one word alone: character. It was during a period several years back, when I was doing a lot of chart readings for individual clients, and doing a lot of writing workshops, that I started to notice something.

The key to the hidden parts of a person's nature can often be found in the eighth house of the chart. I think of this as the "sex and money" house. Sometimes the eighth house is called "the house of secrets." When it comes to these two subjects, there is a level of repression, guardedness, and opaqueness I find quite fascinating.

The Sex-and-Money Workshop

Writers, by nature, are a nosy bunch. Like detectives, we thrive on secrets. We love to know what makes people tick. Curiosity, people! If we are not curious about our characters, their darkest secrets, why would anyone else be?

In my workshops, we do a little exercise called "Sex and Money." That's when the things really get wild. So open a window, throw your inhibitions aside, and let's begin with sex, shall we? What you are being called upon to do here is to choose a character from your piece and do some free-writing to explore the intimate areas of this person's life.

See if you can write about your character's sexual persona. Skip the obvious. It's not what he looks like or how he describes himself; it's what he consciously or unconsciously holds back, keeps to himself. If you have to state the superficial just to warm up, fine. But quickly turn up the heat, and go deep. (Note to Janet Jackson: I'm available for songwriting on your next CD.) Ask yourself, at the very end of the exercise, "What do I *still* not know about who this person is as a sexual being?"

When you do this exploration, remember: your character, just like anyone else, keeps certain things hidden. What you want to do is get to the complex parts of her sexual nature that she's never revealed to her lover, her best friend, probably even herself.

Vanity is often a big clue. Your character's, sure. Perhaps he is vain about his body and embarrassed to be such a metrosexual. But what is even more key is *your* vanity.

I've seen many a writer, especially folks working on characters who are their alter-egos, or their muses, create people on the page who are fantasy objects, characters they wish they could be, or wish they could be with. How boring those characters are to readers! Think of it this way. You have a friend who is newly involved with someone. Infatuation is in full throttle. All this friend tells you is how great the object of his or her affection is, how sexy, how passionate, how compassionate, how funny, etc. How boring!

As a writer you need to go deeper into your character and find the paradoxes, the details, the complexity. And the subject of sex will lead you there. But only if you approach this as a piece of investigative journalism, not as a fluff piece.

So put your investigative journalist hat on and work through this exercise. Just make sure it's a sexy 1940s film noir hat, maybe even a snood (oh, how I love that word).

Exercise: Sexual Intuition

(No, it's not the name of my new perfume—but it does rhyme with it.)

1. Pick a character from your piece and write for five minutes, completely uncensored, about this person's sexual nature. Seek out secrets and qualities that would truly surprise even this character's closest friend.

2. Ask yourself "What am I still not getting about this character's sexual persona and attitudes about sex?"

3. Take another few minutes and write about the nature of this character's intimacy issues (everyone's got 'em). Be specific.

4. What sexual image does he or she try to project? Why?

5. How are you similar to this character, different?

6. You may ... er ... *do* as many characters as you like.

Money Changes Everything

If you think people are secretive about sex and sexuality, try taking a peek into anyone's bills and bank statements. More than sex even, money can be the area where power and shame issues combine to turn your character's head into a labyrinth of nameless fears and misplaced desires. (Actually, that's not a bad name for a law firm. "Nameless Fears and Misplaced Desires, may I help you?")

In this exercise, your job is to try to uncover your character's hidden issues around money. Control probably came up in the sexual exercise, and it could here, too. But the details around the control issues are what we are looking for. Appearance probably plays a key role, too. You've had some foreplay working on the sexual questions; now it's time for the money shot!

Exercise: Follow the Money

1. Pick a character from your piece and write for five minutes, completely uncensored, about this person's financial habits. Seek out secrets and qualities that would truly surprise even this character's closest friend.

2. Ask yourself, "What am I still not getting about this character's attitudes and actions in regards to money?"

3. Take another few minutes and write about the nature of this character's financial woes (everyone's got 'em). Be specific.

4. What financial image does he or she try to project? Why?

5. How are you similar to this character, different?

6. Try this with as many characters as you like.

Now that you know the moves, let's change the subject to one that's even more personal: dough!

Exercise: Dirty Sexy Money

1. Take five minutes to write about the connections you see between your character's attitudes toward sex and attitudes toward money.

2. Write about what you think is most difficult about being this character, living his life. Get under his skin and reveal what is most pleasurable, most threatening to him.

3. In which area of his life is this character most apt to show some growth, some positive change—sex or money (no crass jokes, please)? Why? What makes the other area harder to deal with?

Fascinating answers to these questions always arise in workshops. And when writers really make an attempt to get under the skin of their characters, using these exercises, a great deal of empathy arises. A deeper understanding that may not have been there before. That is what this third step, "nurture," is all about. If you maintain the attitude that you already know everything there is to know about your character, or that you know him well enough, you are cutting off the potential for a deeper connection. Break through your own inhibitions, honey, and don't be afraid to truly *know* your people. If you are too bored or smug to do this, then don't be surprised if your readers are too bored or smug to engage with your work at all.

Whew, it's getting hot in here isn't it? And we are not quite done yet ...

Get to the Essence

If I had to choose one key word to capture the essence of this chapter, it would have to be: intimacy.

This is the stage of the writing process that calls for you to form a deeper, more connected relationship with your writing, with your characters. Just like in real relationships, you may say to yourself, "Yes, that's exactly what I want to do ... but how?"

Well, you've already done a lot by delving into the most deeply personal areas of your characters' lives—sex and money. But now, you need to do something different. Find the essence of who your character is, and see how you as a person connect to that spirit. And you can do it with one word. What that one word is depends upon your character.

Several years ago, I read a terrific book by Czech author Milan Kundera, called *The Art of the Novel*. In one section, he describes the process he went through in developing the character of Tereza in his lauded novel *The Unbearable Lightness of Being*. In thinking about Tereza, Kundera suggests that one of the keys to this character's nature could be found in the word *vertigo*. By (as he put it), interrogating the word, he imagined he could come to understand vertigo, come to understand Tereza.

Kundera says all of his books are meditative interrogations. And by pushing more deeply, more specifically to discover what the word *vertigo* really means, and how it connects to Tereza, Kundera reveals a micro example of how the macro of his novels is constructed.

"Characters are not made up people, they are experimental selves," Kundera says.

In reading about his process, you really come to believe this quote. After all, Tereza, a submissive, domesticated woman, seems nothing like the macho, alpha-male author. Yet in his discussion of his writing, we also see clearly that Kundera's aim was not to try to understand a kind of woman like Tereza, someone outside himself, but rather to understand the part of himself that *is* Tereza.

This emotionally connected way of creating art reminds me of a profile I read of filmmaker Pedro Almodóvar in *The New York Times Magazine*. The cover story, written by Lynn Hirschberg, was published to coincide with the release of his film *Bad Education*. That film, which dealt in part with the sexual relationship between a young boy and a priest, led Hirschberg to ask Almodóvar if the film was autobiographical.

"Anything that is not autobiographical is plagiarism," he responded.

Indeed! In these literal times that we live in, it would have been easy for the Spanish auteur to have responded with a "yes," validating our literal, obvious way of thinking, or with a "no" or "no comment," closing off conversation. Instead, he responded like a true artist by basically expressing this: an artist must be able to empathize with, to understand, at least in a small way, the pieces as well as the whole of his creation. And in some way, small or large, the artist is his character.

Sometimes one word can help you to key into the deepest parts of your character. Remember "Rosebud"!

Exercise: One Word

1. Choose a character from your piece. Intuitively pick one word that captures that character's essence. Clearly, we could all be described by many words. The challenge is to focus on just one. Make sure to choose a word that has some specificity to it, some juice. Recently, I did this exercise with a client. She had two words in mind: *intense* and *frenetic*. Luckily, she went with the latter, which has more precision to it, than the former, which could describe so many of us so much of the time. Remember, "frenetic" trumps "intense."

2. Riff off the word you chose by interrogating it and yourself. What does your word mean? What are your first associations with that word? Why are you so interested in it? What does this word have to do with your character?

3. What is it you hope to discover about yourself by tapping into the meaning of your one word?

Kudos, Kiddo(s)!

You looked deeply into the psyche of your character and uncovered her hidden attitudes toward sex and money.

You made connections between how she views both of those volatile subjects.

You searched and found one word to capture the essence of your character.

This was not Character Algebra, my dears; oh, no, it was Advanced Character Calculus at the very least!

14

psychological types

Several years ago, while working part-time as a counselor at the AIDS Hotline in New York City, my friend Jim asked me to do a favor for him. He was studying for his Doctor of Psychology degree and needed volunteers to submit to a five-hour personality test, Rorschachs and all. "After I've studied your responses," Jim said, with a mischievous look. "I'll diagnose you!"

That was all I needed to hear. I agreed to be a guinea pig, all in the hopes of finding out what type of sicko I really was (sorry ... I am)! One Saturday afternoon he came to my apartment armed with several folders filled with questionnaires, and a big blank yellow legal pad upon which to note my responses. By the time it was over I was haunted by spiders doing push-ups, impressed by my own short-term memory, and disturbed by my lack of spatial skill.

Several months later he'd completed his project and set up a
meeting with me to discuss the results and give me my diagnosis. Over cappuccino he sugar-coated the findings. "The point
of the study was to determine your defense mechanisms ... and
by nature, there are no 'good defense mechanisms'. They all
sound rather negative."

I'll save his actual findings till the end; by then you'll already
have diagnosed all your characters, along with yourself, your
family, and friends.

Dig Into the Psyche

Understanding your characters on a deeper level is essential if
you want your readers/audience to connect with them. One of
the keys to your character's psyche may be found in his or her
defense mechanisms. Although we all, as humans, share certain traits, some of us swing more in one direction than another.
The same is true of our characters.

And so, here are nine psychological types, for your consider-
ation. Bear in mind that these are all different types of internal
defense mechanisms. What is fascinating about them is that
they may not be obvious, people may not wear their defenses
like a pair of neon socks. We all dip in and out of many of these
defenses all the time. Depending on the situation we all behave
in a depressed or narcissistic way sometimes.

The "types" refer to the primary defense mechanism that each
person uses as a default response, regardless of external circumstances. Also, there are many degrees to each defense from
functional to neurotic to psychotic! Someone could have a
slightly compulsive drive that he can integrate into a normal
day-to-day life or be compulsive in an extreme way, veering into

severe mental illness. For most of us these defenses are subtle, almost invisible to the casual observer.

1. Schizoid Personality Defense

   The schizoid type is prone to fantasy, withdrawal, hyper-sensitivity, and receptivity, and fears engulfment more than anything else. The schizoid needs to hide within his own head, but sometimes finds it very lonely there, so he pulls others into close, cocoonlike relationships, shutting out the scary real world. He experiences a constant push-pull cycle between wanting intense closeness and feeling an intense need for space. When pushed against the wall, his need for complete autonomy and space trumps his need for closeness, but generally his life is all about the struggle between the two extremes.

2. Paranoid Personality Defense

   The paranoid is driven by a deep fear of being humiliated. She is always expecting this humiliation to come, and unconsciously seeks out confirmation of her paranoid fantasies. She tends to induce the reaction she fears most. Paranoids need a lot of eye contact and reassurance that the listener agrees with her extreme view of herself and the world. This type is often plagued by shame and guilt over the overaggressive, powerful part of her nature. She may project this aggressiveness onto others whom she fears being persecuted by.

3. Narcissistic Personality Defense

   There are two types of narcissists. Empty narcissists feel an extreme emptiness, a vague sense of being false, inferior, incomplete, accompanied usually by shame and envy.

Grandiose narcissists experience a compensatory self-importance, vanity, superiority. Narcissists view others as extensions of themselves, not as separate human beings. Empty narcissists need others to fill them up. Grandiose narcissists need others to mirror them and provide constant reinforcement.

4. Hysterical (Histrionic) Personality Defense

Hysterics tend to exaggerate intense feelings in a theatrical way in an attempt to protect against being humiliated for having those feelings. They are likely to make a big, inappropriate show of mocking themselves, rather than wait for someone else to mock them. They fear the mercurial nature of powerful people in their lives who may sometimes be kind, sometimes cruel.

5. Psychopathic Personality Defense

The psychopathic (also known as sociopathic) personality possesses a primitive envy: the desire to destroy that which he desires most. He lacks emotional experience with love or empathy and is driven by the desire to exert power over others, but often expresses this drive in subtle, masked ways. The psychopath is very seductive and capable of reading others and telling them what they want to hear ... but then turning on a dime and becoming extremely cold and cruel.

6. Obsessive-Compulsive Personality Defense

This type exerts a rigid need for control and a strong desire to keep more animalistic feelings at bay by acting as an upright citizen. The obsessive-compulsive is defined by the belief that controlling one's thoughts and behavior can control outcomes in a chaotic world. She tends to be very self-critical of her own "immoral" or sadistic thoughts. These types are often heavily prone to intellectualization and emotionally going "blank."

7. Depressive and Manic Personality Defense

   These types are driven by a belief in their inner badness. Their losses and rejections are attributed to some inner lack or having "driven people away." They are extremely self-critical and sometimes driven to help others in order to feel worthy and good.

8. Masochistic (Self-Defeating) Personality Defense

   Like depressives, they believe they are supposed to be punished because they are bad. However, this type also derives some pleasure from the moral superiority they feel over their victimizers because they (the masochists) do not give in to the urge to express aggression.

9. Dissociative Personality Defense (or Multiple Personality)

   In these types, the personality is fractured into multiple selves, each one serving a different function. They are usually the victims of real trauma and have mastered the ability to "shut off" a feeling or a side of themselves that is too threatening to experience; while in a dissociative state, they take on the personality of one of their "alters" (alternate personalities).

Now it is time to put pen to paper. This exercise can be played with your writing workshop group, a buddy, or solo.

Exercise: Psychological Types

Preparation: You've already read descriptions of nine psychological types. Now take a sheet of paper and rip it up into nine pieces. On each piece write down the numbers one through nine. Toss them into a hat. As always, light a candle, close your eyes, and breathe deeply for a few minutes, and then begin. When you begin writing, do not stop until time is up; let your unconscious lead you and just keep your pen moving on the page.

1. Pick a number from the hat and read about the corresponding personality type. After reading it, ask yourself which of your characters seems most like this type. Pretend you are a detective trying to clue into your character's hidden motivations.

2. When you are done, pass the number of your type to the person to your left. The person on your right will pass you the number of her type. If you are working alone, just draw another number. Now pretend that another character, someone who reminds you of this other type, has run into your first character on a train. Take another five minutes to write down a scene between these two characters.

3. Pick a third number from the hat and think of a corresponding character from your piece. What would happen if this person entered the scene? Play out the triangular dynamic and see where it takes you.

4. Write down some concise notes describing what you learned from the above experiment. How can you apply it to your project, next time you sit down to write?

Heck, you're sitting down already, why not write a little bit more right now? You can handle half an hour, can't you? Add this time to your writing hours and then reward yourself with a cup of joe, a shot of whiskey, or an extra session with your shrink. After this exercise you'll need it!

Final Unmasking

Now for the big reveal: Jim told me I was schizoid, and then he said it was okay; he's schizoid, too. We had a moment of closeness, then a moment of distance. He referred me to the book *Psychological Diagnosis: Understanding Personality Structure in the Clinical Process* by Dr. Nancy McWilliams, upon which the findings were based. Dr. McWilliams, president of the Division of Psychoanalysis of the American Psychological Association, is incredibly insightful and in tune with the creative mind. I wrote to her and asked her for her further thoughts on the torment that all writers seem to go through.

She said, "I think writers come in all personality types, but schizoid seems to me by far the most common: the artistic temperament, the right-brained tendencies, the sensitivity … especially fiction writers, because of the importance of the imagination to schizoid people."

Her book (which she is currently updating) was a riveting read, and I found myself recognizing family and friends in her personality types right away. I read the schizoid section and never felt more understood in my life! If you want to truly understand your characters, their motivations, fears, and defenses, keep playing this little game. Best-case scenario: you will create a richer, deeper, more nuanced character-based work of art. Worst-case scenario: off to the loony bin! (But hey, that's where your mega-hit memoir may begin ….) Whatever you do, you can be sure that by engaging more deeply with your characters, you will nurture your relationship to them, ensuring that your readers will connect deeply as well.

And McWilliams says Henry James was a schizoid type, too. So there!

Kudos, Kiddo(s)!

You learned a little about the hidden defense mechanisms that each of us unconsciously uses.

You applied this knowledge to some of your characters, to get a better sense of their psyches.

You observed your characters interacting with other characters, and gained deeper insight into these relationships.

That was a lot of work. Retreat to the couch, sans shrink, *with* snacks.

15

writing in reverse

When Roger Angell, esteemed memoirist, chronicler of baseball, and fiction editor at the *New Yorker*, came to speak to my writing class at the New York University School of Journalism, he said he wasn't much of a believer in spending a lot of time suffering over your lead; instead he thought about his last line, and worked backward.

Author John Irving (*The World According to Garp, The Cider House Rules,* too many glorious books to mention) also begins with the end. He has spoken often about planning the direction of his novels in his mind, usually for a few months. Then he writes the very last sentence. From there he works backward to the beginning.

Angell and Irving are not alone in their focus on the end. To explore the ways to write in reverse, let's start at the end, with two of my clients who used the exercise in different ways.

Beginning at the End

I asked my client and friend Lauren Yaffe, who was working on a screenplay, to try this exercise, to figure out how to connect the scenes in her script so they flowed properly. Afterward, here's what she said:

Lauren

At one point in my screenplay, my main character rallies his school teammates to go searching for water to save their town when up until this point, he had never showed the least inkling of interest in working with his teammates or helping his town. Though I felt confident about the scenes of him stuck in his ways (leading up to the town water crisis), and had a good draft of what followed once he set about on the water search, I continually choked whenever I tried to write the scenes in between. I knew certain scenes I wanted in there, but wasn't sure if they *needed* to be in there and why, and how they all fit together and led logically to the water search.

Jill had me try an exercise of writing the scenes in reverse. The logic went like this: "D and his team go to search for water because …" I had to answer the question with the previous scene. The previous scene started with the action: "D and his team return to school to find that the principal is calling for a town evacuation." I then had to connect the dots of that scene so that the end of it (D going on the water search) would make sense: "D and his team go to search for water because when they return to school to find the principal calling for evacuation, they …"

This reverse progression forced me to explore my own logic for the story differently. Sequencing the scenes in reverse—really, effect and cause—served as checks and balances for what scenes were necessary and in what order. I had to justify in my own mind that the principal's evacuation caused a change in D that made him then change his behavior.

Now, one would think that writing a scene with such a clear end in mind could make for stagnant writing, but it had the opposite effect for me. For one, I felt more of a sense of urgency to get from the beginning of the scene to the end. Also, phrasing the question in this way, "D goes to search for water because of the evacuation," created a mystery for me, as the writer, which was then exciting to solve. When I asked the question that way, my first response was that of someone who knew nothing of the story: "Really? How does the evacuation have that effect?" Another reaction was, "Hmm. How did I get D to that decision?" So it was then exciting to me to be able to prove my logic was sound by showing it in a way that made sense.

I asked fiction writer Jennifer Neal to write a sentence describing the end of her story, then the same for the middle of her story, and the same for the beginning, and then to try to fill in the gaps. Here's her report.

Jennifer

The result of the first exercise was a Eureka moment. I realized that I could just write the whole thing in a series of loose sentences and "fill them out" into pages or paragraphs. For someone as organized as myself this seemed like the way forward. It's one thing to just write and write, but quite another to write to a template. I've always given in to the temptation to edit as I write and this exercise suited me perfectly. Plus, it all seemed too easy. For the first time, I saw what it might look like when finished.

Every story has a beginning, middle and end. Homing in on those points in the narrative could be very fruitful.

Exercise: Effect and Cause

1. Write three long sentences: one describing the end scene of your story, one describing a key middle scene, and finally, one describing your opening scene.

2. Work backward to come up with single sentences that fill in the gaps. Keep asking yourself, "Why?" (As in, if in the final scene Bill and Jane decide not to divorce, why? What might've occurred in the scene right before?) If you get stuck fill in a "placeholder"; just remind yourself you can come up with something better later.

3. Now read over what you've written from beginning to end and note where there are gaps in logic. Work on those during your writing hours.

Slow Down

Henry James once said that readers like to watch characters suffer. He did not mean this in the sadistic sense. Rather, we are all human beings, and there is a comfort and sense of connection when we observe the private moments in a character's trajectory. I've seen many prose writers write as if they were writing screenplays: focused only on action and dialogue, not the subtle, torturous (yet mundane, banal) moments of human existence. Even scriptwriters, who need to write "lean and mean" can benefit from taking the time to stay with their characters in slow motion; it's a wonderful way to truly get under their skin. Writing slowly is an art. You don't have to be The Master himself, however, to practice it. Get out your pencil and begin.

Exercise: Henry James
Slow **Writing in Reverse**

1. Write a moment late in your story, as the end of your tale draws near, and move through this scene as slowly as you can … even slower still! When you are done, try writing a scene that might've occurred right before this one. Now how about doing one more … slowly …?

2. While you are in this Henry James mode: take a very small incident that you experienced or witnessed in the last 48 hours and "give it" to one of your characters. (Example: on a crowded train or bus you saw a very mismatched couple holding hands and chatting. One of them reminded you of a person from your past.) Slowly weave in this scene to your story. *Then* write another slow scene showing what happened before this.

Add a Hint of Music

Jeremy Seaver came to my workshop one fine fall and left me a beautiful gift—an envelope full of piano sheet music, arranged for beginners, and a lovely letter. He said that he, too, had taken up the piano as an adult, purely for the joy of it, and that playing some of these beautiful jazz and swing standards, even at "the level of a five-year-old," brought him great happiness. It was a kindred spirit moment. It took me a year to learn "My Funny Valentine," but what a wonderful year.

Recently, I've moved on to sight reading and am taking a crack at my one of my favorite composers: Burt Bacharach. For a non-musician beginner this is tough stuff, but oh so joyous. My partner Anne (a lifelong pianist, who taught me my first chords) bought me an "easy piano" Bacharach book for my birthday.

During my piano lesson, I asked my teacher/guru, Ed Pastorini, to give me a hand with it. I spent a good 15 minutes on the first measure of "This Guy's in Love with You." I kept trying to move on, but found myself saying, "Let me go back … all the way back." To which Ed would say, "Go back all the way to the primordial ooze." (We do have fun, Edzo and I, 'tis true.)

I went to sleep that night dreaming about it (with *The Complete Idiot's Guide to Music Theory*, also from Anne, in my hands).

That was a long intro to a short exercise.

"Burt Bacharach—One Measure"

1. Think of a sentence as a measure of music. Spend 15 minutes, "playing" that sentence. Play around with it. Give it different rhythms, punctuation. Memorize it. Repeat it like a mantra in your head. Tonight, go to sleep with it.

Tweak the End

Exercise: Final Image

1. Imagine a final image for your story. Write it out in one simple, elegant sentence.

2. Now riff off that image. Expand it into a two-paragraph meditation.

Flannery O'Connor, I was taught, wrote her fiction in complete forward motion. No plan or outline. But then she went back and found an interesting thread, an image, and found a way to weave that image in three separate times within the body of the piece.

3. Take an image (either the final one you just wrote on or something else), and write it into an end scene in your piece, a middle scene and a beginning scene.

Exercise: Final Sentence

1. Write the final sentence of your piece.

2. Just as an experiment, write a new first sentence for your story. See if you can subtly, invisibly, embed the inevitable conclusion of your story that can be found in your final sentence into your opening sentence.

3. Now imagine your first sentence is your last sentence. With that in mind, create a completely new first sentence.

4. Write four more possible final sentences. Think of each of them as completely different "colors," meaning: don't just tweak the same sentence four different ways, but really come up with totally new end lines.

Keep Your Readers in the Mix

Now that we're reached the end of this chapter, I'd like to return to the beginning. I mentioned Mr. Angell's visit to my New York University feature writing class. When one of my students asked him if he could give one piece of advice to young writers, what would it be, here's what he said:

"Remember the reader."

He made sure I wrote it on the blackboard in big, bold letters:

REMEMBER THE READER.

In the spirit of "writing in reverse," let's imagine that you have completed your work. Your dream comes true and you see it published. Complete strangers have the chance to buy your book. Now the question ... why? Have you considered the reader's experience? A question I think is extremely helpful to ask yourself is this:

What is the feeling I want to induce in the reader?

If your end result is ultimately to give the reader a particular kind of satisfying reading experience, keep that in mind from the beginning.

If you remember the reader from end to beginning, beginning to end, you will have done your job. Regardless of the result. All you have to do is check in from time to time and ask yourself, "Am I doing anything right now that might be 'taking the reader out' of the reading experience?" Just by asking that question you are doing a great service to your reader and to yourself. Remember, the reader is not your mom or your best bud.

If, *in the end*, you would like to form a connection with many people, not just the ones in your inner circle, then remember these three little words: remember the reader. If you've forgotten the reader, no worries; it is never too late in this draft and revision process to reverse yourself.

Kudos, Kiddo(s)!

You experimented with writing backward and hopefully discovered it was so much more than a con man's trick!

You did some slooooow writing in reverse, and really got a chance to be in the text, and find more texture.

You imagined a final image and a final sentence for your work. That's *epitathfastic*, baby!

You have begun to truly remember the reader. Forgetting the reader is the biggest hindrance for most writers. Now you are strong enough to see that you can find a balance between writing for yourself and remembering the reader. They are not mutually exclusive.

step 4

go

Finish and let your project go, so it can exist in the real world.

16

do the opposite

You are almost at the end. It seems like long ago that you *began* with your best idea, and you *arranged* your work into a concrete form. You *nurtured* your project with love. And now it is time to do final work needed, to let your project *go* and exist in the real world.

First, let's be honest. Your goal right now is to simply *meet* your goal. If you set out to write a draft of a short story, say 5,000 words, focus only on getting that draft done. However, if life has thrown you a myriad of obstacles (excuses, excuses, darling!), readjust your goal. If you have to take it down a notch, so be it. Hopefully you can meet and exceed your goal, but the point is this: just keep going, no matter what.

When you have met your goal, then of course you will need to come up with your next goal. You will probably have to write many drafts of your piece; and if you are working on a full-length project you may need to work for much longer to get it to the point when it is ready to be released into the real world. But the only way to get to that final destination is to keep setting mini-goals for yourself. Like mini-donuts, these mini-goals can and should become addictive, Homer (I'm addressing the gluttonous Mr. Simpson as well as the author of *The Odyssey*).

In the beginning of this process, you probably had a grandiose vision of what you could do, and now perhaps you have discovered that doing something small and well is enough for right now. Not only enough, but far superior to giving in to the strong impulse to undo the whole thing by blowing off your whole project. Of course that impulse is strong. It would be so much easier to walk away than to find a way to keep going.

The theme of this chapter is to "Do the Opposite," the opposite of your every impulse. Like most of the tricks of the trade that I've shared with you in *Bang the Keys*, do the opposite emerged from high literature *and* pop culture. What does Carl Jung have in common with George Costanza from *Seinfeld*? The Shadow knows, my dears!

Bizarro Meets Jung

Let's start with *Seinfeld*. There was a particularly brilliant episode of the hit '90s sitcom in which George Costanza realized that his every impulse, instinct, and action inevitably led him toward failure and humiliation. As an experiment he decided to "Do the Opposite" in the hopes of achieving better results. Next thing you know, this neurotic schlemiel got the girl, the career, the works!

Perhaps like the usual George, you usually listen to the slacker voice in your head telling you that you might as well troll around the Internet, hang out on your couch, or get into petty squabbles with your colleagues, friends, and the like. If you do the opposite, you may actually decide to take some steps toward professionalizing yourself as a writer. That means working, baby—doing your writing hours and staying later to do some more, rather than concocting harebrained schemes to avoid doing your work.

Imagine the "Bizarro George" on one shoulder telling you to do the opposite, and Carl Jung sitting on your other shoulder suggesting that you embrace your shadow. Jung might advise you to look into the aspects of your work that make you uncomfortable, and rather than run from them, run toward them. Express the shadow part of your writer's personality, rather than repress it.

In my workshops, and my private coaching work, I've seen this issue come up again and again. Writers are so uptight about how their work is going to be perceived (before it's even written!) that they panic at the thought of writing prose or scripts that are too …

- Melodramatic

- Offensive

- Humorless

- Superficial

- Obvious

- Unoriginal

- Obscure

- Sexist or some other "ist" or "obic"

The same is true for writers who are afraid of offending their family and friends, or offending the public at large. I can't tell you how many memoirists, and even fiction writers, I've worked with who live in fear of what their loved ones are going to say about them. The funny thing is this: writers are destined to be misunderstood no matter what they do. We can't win!

If you are terrified that your father is going to be offended by the scene in your personal essay in which you describe him arguing with your mother, and making some nasty remarks, sure, your fears may be justified. He may get angry. But he also may appreciate the efforts you took to show the *other* parts of his nature: his humor, his passion for life, etc. That's only if you have done your job and created a three-dimensional version of him on the page, not just an easy target for your childhood resentments.

But even if you are writing fiction and you take (as all writers do) bits and pieces from your own emotional experiences, your loved ones and the public are extremely likely to misread you. If you are Latino and now married to a black woman, but had a two-year relationship with a Korean woman in college, you can best believe that the Asian love interest in your novel will be interpreted as your real-life college lover. Even if you only took five percent (the Asian part) from her, and really developed this character based on a composite of two other relationships and (insert sound of a gong here) your imagination!

Maybe your ex-lover herself will even be flattered by your portrayal of her, even though your character had almost nothing to do with her. Maybe your ex-lover was a prankster and you took that personality trait and "gave" it to a white frat-boy character.

No matter what you write, you risk being misinterpreted, so why not take that as an excuse to take some *real* risks, by writing without inhibition, as if no one will read your work, knowing that you can polish it and pull back some of the glaring flaws later? (Note to my Asian buds: don't hate me because I love the image and sound of the gong! I watched too many episodes of Chuck Barris's *The Gong Show* at an impressionable age.)

Serve Your Words with Power

And while we are bringing up iconic images of the '70s, I have three words for you: Billie Jean King. When I was doing a series of workshops a few years back *and* taking tennis lessons, a friend lent me a terrific, kitschy-looking book by the tennis star and feminist heroine, Ms. King. Although the book had a tacky '70s cover, the words within were graceful and meaningful. In writing about tennis for beginners, King made a key point. She said that she watched many beginning players make the mistake of trying to serve with precision. She advised that it is so much more important for tennis players who are developing their game to serve *with power*, with as much force as they can. The precision can come later.

King highly recommended serving with passion and not holding back one iota, with the understanding that it is much easier to develop good aim later, after you've mastered a powerful serve. But to do the opposite, to serve precisely but cautiously, will make it near impossible for you to "add in" power later.

Actors and singers know this, too. Sometimes you have to belt out a crazy performance and risk embarrassment, knowing that later you can refine your work.

So if you are tempted to try and write something that is consciously brilliant, cool, funny, etc. and you are so inhibited by the desire to look good and get it right that you can't seem to break through to your best writing, why not do the opposite?

Some folks hate hearing their voices on tape. But after a while they get over it. You will, too!

Exercise: Voices Carry

1. You hate a particular voice or style you are writing in (too melodramatic, too racy, too esoteric, etc.). Instead of telling this voice to "Hush Hush" (thanks, Aimee Mann!), give yourself permission to belt it out. The first step is to identify this voice. Write a paragraph describing what it is about this particular voice or style of writing of yours that you find so distressing.

2. Take 5 to 10 minutes to write a scene from your project that completely indulges that voice. Go mad with it!

3. Read over what you just wrote and see if you can find one sentence or phrase from what you just banged out that you really have appreciation for.

4. Now use that as a starting point to write a new little ditty for your story, this time keeping "that voice" in balance. Don't try to suppress the voice that you hate, but don't go all the way with it either.

5. What's the takeaway message for you? Write down your response in one to two sentences.

Opposing Attitudes

The Buddha taught of the eight vicissitudes of human existence:

- Gain and loss

- Fame and ill repute

- Praise and blame

- Pleasure and pain

When we are deeply attached to a state of being—"I've lost everything ... it's over for me"—we may just experience a gain, the next minute, the next month, two years from now. Nothing is permanent. And yet, as human beings we are constantly attaching to a feeling, a state of mind, a response (internal or external) as if it is forever.

Exercise: Give Yourself a Vicissitude Adjustment

1. Pick one of the four pairs of "opposites" that you most connect to at this moment. Write for five minutes about one part of the pair. Thinking about yourself as a writer, riff off this concept. For example, why do you connect so strongly to praise? What memory does the word conjure up for you? What emotions?

2. Do the same exercise but this time with the opposite word in the pair.

3. Now pick a pair to which you have the least connection. Write for five minutes (total) about each side of the pair. Why is it that you do not have such strong feelings about (for example) pleasure and pain?

4. Write a paragraph or two giving yourself a bit of Buddha-esque advice in which you help yourself to apply the same level of nonattachment you feel toward the pair of being-states you just wrote about, to the previous pair, for which you still feel a strong emotional charge.

Live Out Your Fairytale

For most of us, fairytales were our introduction to storytelling. Returning to that form could release some of your creative inhibitions.

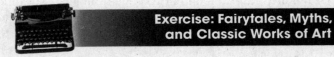

Exercise: Fairytales, Myths, and Classic Works of Art

1. Tap into the hidden grandiosity in your work (and more importantly, its potential for eternal value), and write a synopsis of your story as if it were a fairytale or myth. Begin however you wish, but if in doubt you can try these prompts or a variation on them:

   "Once upon a time ..."

   "There once lived a man ..."

   "It was an era of ..."

2. If your piece is innately a comedy, write a synopsis of it as a tragedy, or vice versa.

3. What fairytale or myth is your story most connected to? Why? What is the moral or value of that myth and of your particular piece?

4. Worried about writing a piece that is similar in some way to a classic work, and different in that your piece completely sucks? Give in to your fear, dear. Write a synopsis of

your story or a bulleted outline of the plot, and purposely adapt it to the structure of the work you admire. Afterward write about what you can learn from the structure of that classic work to apply to your own work in progress.

A Different Point of View

The year 1947 saw the first publication of French author and thinker Raymond Queneau's delicious soufflé of a book: *Exercises in Style*. In it, a narrator relays the tale of his experience on a crowded bus, in which he witnesses one man accusing another of purposely jostling him. The neat trick of this perfect little collection is Queneau's telling of this banal anecdote 99 different ways. In "Hesitation" he begins with the phrase "I don't know" and writes many sentences in the question form. In "Precision" he provides exact measurements of the characters involved, along with many other quantifiable facts. In "Dream" he describes the encounter in surreal terms and ends with this sentence: "I woke up."

Following in Queneau's footsteps, try the following exercise.

> ### Exercise: Queneauing Me, Queneauing You
>
> 1. For best possible results, buy Queneau's *Exercises in Style* and use it for this exercise. But if you are in a hurry, try this: on scraps of paper, write down a bunch of story styles (you can use "Hesitation," "Precision," and "Dream" to get started), and throw them into a hat. Pick one and write a page-and-a-half version of your story (the whole story or just a portion), using that style.
>
> 2. Repeat as necessary.

3. Mix two styles and try again.

4. Write down the "takeaway" for this exercise.

Kudos, Kiddo(s)!

You began your final step. You've come a long way, baby!

You played with opposites and tried on different writing styles.

You have not run from the self-loathing voice in your head but instead have countered it by embracing the writing voice that makes you cringe. And you survived!

After doing a lot of ruminating and a lot of writing exercises, you achieved a greater handle on how to handle all the voices in your head!

17

morning papers

All theater people know the thrill and horror of opening up the morning papers, the day after a show opens. Talk about mood-enhancing or ego-destroying. The words in those reviews hold so much power, at least in the moment. One of the exercises I do in my workshop involves taking the time to actually sit down and write a scathing review of your piece, followed by a glowing one. The beauty of this experience is that you finally allow those nutty voices in your head free rein. Let your harshest critic tear you to bits and pounce upon your every weakness. Let your greatest fan kvell over your every comic moment, and bit of dramatic dialogue. Ultimately, you may find a grain of something useful when you merge the two voices.

The inner critic is like the bogeyman. When we are lying in the dark near an open closet, we may see monsters. When we turn the light on, we see what's really there: a shoetree, some dry cleaning, and a shoebox containing news clippings that reveal our partner to be a crazed lunatic who killed her twin and successfully covered up the murder. Oh, sorry. I was channeling *Single White Female*. I adored that funfest, by the way. Sadly, the critics did not. Viva Barbet!

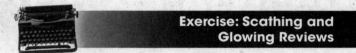

Exercise: Scathing and Glowing Reviews

1. Flash forward in your mind to when your work (whether novel, essay, screenplay, etc.) *is* complete. Write a scathing review in which you tear apart your piece with the passion of a divorce lawyer. Take five minutes; don't censor yourself. If you need more time do another five minutes.

2. Now write a review of the same piece, but this time make it a glowing review. Imagine that the reviewer you are embodying just drank your Kool-Aid and is utterly enraptured by your genius as a writer.

3. Look over the two reviews and write for a few minutes about what you think the constructive "takeaway" is. If you could combine the voices of the two critics, what realistic advice that really resonates with you, might they give?

It's Important Right Now That We Talk, Killer to Killer

For those of you who do not have every line of *All About Eve* memorized, I suggest you rent the flick, and summon up the character of Addison DeWitt, Deliciously Evil Critic Incarnate. Try reading your reviews aloud for full effect!

Laura Esther Wolfson, a well-published essayist, is a soft-spoken, multilingual writer (she also works as a Russian translator at the United Nations). Here, she writes of her nonfiction book:

Laura

Scathing Review

The subject dealt with here—author goes to ancestral shtetl in search of a connection to his/her familial and cultural past—has been covered exhaustively by authors far more talented than Wolfson. This time, however, there is a twist: the trail has gone so cold that there is nothing to find and nothing to tell. Nonetheless, Wolfson manages to fill 60 pages with meandering, unstructured, bloated prose, or perhaps prosiness would be a better word. Every chance encounter is expanded upon until its insignificance becomes excruciating and impossible to ignore. Well-known historical facts are reworked for maximum sentimentality and horror.

In the '70s a reviewer described Meryl Streep in *Sophie's Choice* as yet another actress starving herself in order to play a concentration camp inmate. Wolfson, on the other hand, revisits the Nazi killing fields and finds a big, fat nothing.

Glowing Review

Wolfson handles this familiar material, rife with opportunities for cliché, so masterfully that it grows new in her hands. She follows the path of her grandfather, doing research before she embarks, and she comes up with some startling finds. Her crystalline prose contains echoes of Chekhov and Sholem Aleichem and her tale ranges from an early twentieth-century shtetl in the tsarist empire to late Soviet-era stagnation and post-Soviet euphoria to a house in a university where her father plays Bach and she remembers events she was born too late to experience. This is an intergenerational nonfiction saga of a kind never seen before. Its structure is a masterpiece of post-modernist fragmentation with a story whose richness and heft recalls the masterpieces of nineteenth-century fiction.

My Narrative Brain Trust pal Matt Howe tried the exercise and said "At some point in the process, you must attack your own writing as hard as you can. Think of it as the way consumer products are torture-tested to make sure they'll withstand the rigors of use. If your project has never been tested, how can you hope for it to survive in a very tough marketplace. This was a great, and fun, way to do this.

At first I thought the positive review was BS—useless self-esteem training. But I quickly discovered that writing a rave was as important as a pan. In writing the rave, I had to articulate what my purpose was in writing the book, identify the things I (and thus the fake reviewer) found interesting and compelling about the story. By understanding these aspects of my book, I know what areas I need to bring forward and strengthen.

Overall, I found the fake reviews to be very useful—tools I intend to use over and over as I go forward with my career."

John McCaffrey has been published in *The Norton Anthology of Flash Fiction*, and has just finished writing a novel. He commented, "This exercise is helpful because it forces you to think how a critic might think about your work, which then makes you think how you might (or should) address your self-perceived weaknesses. The problem is that, for me at least, it is easy to find fault in my own work, but putting these flaws in writing seemed almost taboo, as if I was creating a self-fulfilling prophecy of being panned in the future. But in the same yet opposite vein, critiquing a work (as a critic) is also promoting the idea that the work is worthy of criticism (as in, it will be published and read widely). Akin to the old adage that any publicity is good publicity. All in all, I think it is a useful exercise, perhaps for more serious writers, to do on a regular basis."

Criticism That Is Actually Constructive

Remember the famous argument in Beckett's *Waiting for Godot*? The final insult hurled is but one word: critic!

When I write, I try to summon up the critics whom I love best and imagine them advising me. When this works well, it inspires me to please eclectic everyman James Agee with my authenticity, impress Manny Farber with my termite-like pursuit of a humble objective, and satisfy Mrs. Parker with lightness of phrase and depth and emotion. It doesn't always work, but on occasion it works wonders.

Just as the literary heroes we channeled earlier in the book helped us to initially bang the keys and get our work down on paper, our critical heroes can help us as we approach the end. I invite you to find an ideal critic (living or dead, but preferably real, not imaginary), with whom you can internally converse.

I remember reading an incredible piece of film and cultural criticism in *Harper's*, the year after Stanley Kubrick's final film was released. In "Eyes Wide Shut: What the Critics Failed to See in Kubrick's Last Film," Lee Siegel took on his fellow critics and defended a masterpiece (and my favorite movie). For years I carried a worn Xerox of this article around in my bag with me, so that if the subject of *Eyes Wide Shut* ever came up, I wouldn't have to physically attack the person who spewed the obvious, conventional, and utterly bland swill that I and other passionate fans of Kubrick in general, and of this film in particular, were forced to listen to. I wish I were joking, people, but it is true. Just as politics and religion should not be discussed in civilized settings, this film cannot be dissed at a dinner table where I sit, especially if there is a sharp object within reach of my aggressive, impulsive paw!

Basically, Mr. Siegel, a forward-thinking critic, without realizing it, saved some lives. I honestly took the tack of referring people who misread this film and dismissed it, to his *Harper's* article. And it was because of this fine piece of criticism that I began to follow his writing. Last year when *Against the Machine* came out (mentioned in Chapter 6) I was eager to read it, and once again, felt as if I was reading the work of one sane man in the universe. Criticism can be expansive, or nasty, but whatever form it takes, it is part of the life of a writer, whether internalized in that scribe's mind, or externalized in reviews of actual work, or both. The critics must have their voice.

What Have the Critics Taught Us?

And so, the takeaway I leave you with came from my friend Wendy, when she was up at a writer's retreat in Vermont, one winter. I was in the middle of a workshop and asked if she had any advice for my group in regards to the constant presence of self-criticism. She wrote:

> "Someone here had a crit from a visiting artist and he told her he thinks she needs to do something that might embarrass her. We were all talking about what great advice that is … how when you are really willing to go out on a limb and potentially completely humiliate yourself you then have the best chance of doing truly good work.

"There is one poet here who is doing an exercise where she forces herself to write one poem a day. She then carries it around in her pocket and if anyone asks how her work is going she gives it to them to read. She says she does this even if she thinks the day's poem didn't come out very well. She's not going back and editing them; she's just cranking them out. She says she's doing it as an exercise, to kill her 'inner critic'. I don't know how long she is planning to keep this up before she goes back to working intensely on one or two poems, but it sounds like a great exercise to free up one's imagination."

And by the way, I asked Laura for her thoughts on the review exercise (which she originally wrote in Workshop, then e-mailed to me upon request):

"I really enjoyed rereading them, but thought the scathing one was better than the rave."

The critics have spoken!

Kudos, Kiddo(s)!

You faced your worst critic and your greatest supporter, with humor and grace.

You were able to find something useful from all this criticism, something that will serve the work, rather than your ego.

Upon some reflection you began to see how writing reviews of your work (at a late stage in your process) could actually help you to stay true to your vision of your project.

Three cheers and five stars, darlings!

18

time waits for no one

A strange sort of adrenalin kicks in as the end approaches. The week before deadline in my Bang the Keys workshops, it seems that a sudden motivation takes hold. It's one part panic, one part "what the heck," and one part crème de menthe. Oh, wait, that's some 1964 cocktail recipe I came across. Anyway, it's heartening to see that many folks find a way, when there is little time left, to make good use of their time.

To Hell and Back

I admit, I am the opposite of a crammer. I can't stand to procrastinate. I developed my discipline in a very specific way, under very specific conditions. When I first got out of college, I worked in publishing. But I was young, the money was bad, and I knew what I wanted to do: write. However, I came from humble beginnings: cab driver dad, secretary mom, disco queen sister, and French poodle pet—although Gigi actually emerged from pedigree lineage.

I knew I would have to work for a living till I figured out how to make my living as a scribe. This was the early '90s and the AIDS crisis was in full throttle, and affecting my friends, my community, my world, quite directly, quite intensely. I decided that if I had to have a day job, on my way to becoming a *real* writer, I'd feel better knowing that I was doing something with my young, energetic body and spirit to fight the epidemic.

Soon I obtained a position doing very basic public health research, for the New York City Department of Health. My job was to travel to about 10 New York City hospitals, study the medical charts of people diagnosed with AIDS, and make sure that the diagnosis fit the Centers for Disease Control's (often-changing) definition of the illness. I learned a great deal from patients and hospital staff, worked with some incredible people, and felt I was doing a decent, humble job, helping to maintain accurate statistics during an out-of-control epidemic.

After one year, though, I felt a desire to work with people, to counsel, as I'd done ad-hoc for so many years already, first as a college student, then as a volunteer at the Gay and Lesbian Switchboard in New York City. It was at this time that I made a career move that nearly cost me my sanity: I went to work for a large AIDS nonprofit with a very bad rep on the street. Even though every single young colleague of mine who either had worked there, or knew someone who'd worked there, advised me: "Don't do it!" But I was misguided by the innocence and arrogance of youth and had to find out for myself. For the purposes of this anecdote, let's call this place … Hell!

Everyone has their Hell! It's the place you go to work with the best intentions, often when you're very young, and it is there that you discover that *the world is a cesspool.* I had a misguided sense of my own ability to change the unchangeable, and more than that, I had lost my way. I was a writer, not a destroyer of evildoers! But so consumed was I with the injustice all around me, 10 A.M. to 6 P.M. every day, that I stayed in Hell! for 26 months, thinking that I and my outraged buddies could put out the fire. We couldn't. We provided comfort to people who were suffering and dying, but we couldn't douse all those nauseating flames.

I started to plan my escape. I remembered that I was a writer. And so I forced myself to develop a writer's schedule, something I'd never done before. After returning home from work at 6:30 P.M., I fixed a simple supper, and sat down to work from 7 to 10 P.M. I worked on one of those pre-PC word processors. My mother and sister had bought me one for my birthday. It resembled a microwave with a detachable keyboard. Very *Space 1999.* And on it I worked. Every weeknight, no matter what. What I worked on at the time was not of lasting value; I was too immersed in my rage at *the man.* I didn't write a great piece of work during this phase of my life, but I did learn discipline.

I quit Hell! and worked as a DJ and a freelance writer to support myself, but soon returned to the New York City Department of Health, this time as a counselor on the AIDS Hotline. It was a blessing. I worked part-time (with benefits!) alongside a wonderful mix of people, and was able to write part-time as well. By the end of the '90s the worst of the epidemic had passed, I'd sold a couple of books to a major press, and it was time for me to begin writing and teaching, and ultimately coaching writers—full-time.

Within weeks of leaving the working world, to work for myself, I became a member of the Writers Room, an urban writers colony in New York City. Going to the Writers Room to do my work *became* my 9 to 5. But if I hadn't desperately needed to bust out of a toxic nonprofit corporation, I might not have learned how to discipline myself.

Lord knows I wasn't born with a strong sense of self-discipline. I remember being in college at the State University of New York in Purchase, in the late '80s, and studying with fellow film majors, actors, and costume and set designers for our Dramatic Structure exam on Aristotle's *Poetics*. We sat up in our little dorm suite cramming all night for our 9:30 A.M. test. It was both comedy and tragedy!

Most of us have had experiences like this. It's finals time in school and we have to immerse ourselves in material that we may or may not have read or studied in the previous weeks. Or it's deadline time at the office and we have to meet our goal or we may lose our livelihood. That well-worn phrase, "necessity is the mother of invention" is true, my dears.

A Nudge over the Edge

I might not have ever had the impetus to make my first workshop happen if it hadn't been for my dear Izzy, a hardscrabble Bronx alley cat. One winter morning I noticed that his normal quacking voice had a strange timbre to it. The vet announced that he had a benign tumor on his thyroid; it needed to be removed through radiation.

All pet owners know the other part of this story: a huge vet bill. I'd been coaching writers for a short time, and trying, half-heartedly, to pull together a workshop. But Izzy's urgent medical problem was all the impetus I needed. Within a few weeks I'd organized a gang of writers, charged them a nominal fee, and immediately signed over the money I'd earned for that first workshop, to the animal hospital. That is how "Bang the Keys" first began. Izzy, along with his fluffy, haughty Maine-coon sidekick, Sasha, became the mascots of those early classes (often snoring loudly as writers wrote—the first critics)!

I tell you all this because I think we all know what we are capable of when we are put under pressure.

Just as I've been in the process of finishing this book, my pal Wendy has been finishing her film. We recently checked in with each other and I told her that it's been going well but the deadline is a very tight one. She told me that she had just come across a quote from Leonard Bernstein, "to achieve great things, two things are needed, a plan, and not quite enough time." I think this is true. There is never enough time to do things perfectly. But there is enough time to do things well, with skill and with wonder. The clock is part of life, and just as it seems to tick faster as we age and slide toward death, so it does when a deadline approaches.

When there is an urgent time-sensitive matter before us, we are likely to *finally* stop screwing around and get to work. And now that time has come. We've got one chapter left, the clock is ticking, the deadline is at dawn (well, you know what I mean), and if ever there was a time to conjure up the gods of writing inspiration and motivation it is now!

As the Rolling Stones noted in the '60s, "Time Waits for No One"! But let's go back even further in time to the '80s—that wasn't a typo; I mean the *1*580s: that was when the controversial

Italian philosopher Giordano Bruno wrote a work of philosophical fiction, *Candlemaker*, in which a hooker speaks earthy words meant to illuminate a more cosmically heavy belief: "Whoever waits for time is wasting time. If I wait for time, time won't wait for me." You don't have to be a full-lipped rocker, a Neapolitan prostitute, or a contrarian philosopher who was ultimately burned at the stake in Rome (so threatening were his ideas) to connect to those words. And to take them as a signal to write … now!

As we approach the end, you must become comfortable with being your own teacher, the boss of you, if you will.

Exercises: Letters and Roads

1. To warm up for this last stretch, write down 10 quick bullet points reminding yourself how you have met deadlines or performed under pressure in your work life and your personal life. Be as concrete as possible. You could include things like how you prepared for a big meeting, your wedding, a child's graduation party, anything that had a concrete deadline attached to it.

2. The Assignment Letter

   In journalism, when a feature is assigned, a good editor will usually write up an assignment letter and e-mail it to his writer, especially if it's his first time working with that writer. The best editors are the best communicators. They know that if they lay out what they are looking for, clearly and unambiguously, up front, they are much more likely to get it, and more. They possess the respectful, pro-writer soul of Max Perkins (who discovered and nurtured Hemingway and Fitzgerald) mixed with the deadline-crazy toughness of J. Jonah Jameson (Peter Parker's editor at the *Daily Bugle* in the *Spider-Man* comics).

Your job now is to pretend you are your own editor. Adjust the concept to the reality of where you are now. If you have 10 more pages to write, or the last third of your story, or whatever is left—come up with a short assignment letter to yourself, and lay out in real terms what needs to get done, and when. Now take the techniques you recalled in the last exercise and adapt them to your current situation. Afterward, pare down your letter into a short, clear plan that will ensure you will meet your deadline.

3. The Long and Winding Road

I gave you a bittersweet taste of my own journey through Hell! Now give me yours. Write a pared-down and primal version of your own long and winding road. You are here now, with a deep desire to finish your writing project, to be a writer, not just talk about being one. What gates of hell did you have to walk through to get to where you sit now? And what bits of wisdom have you culled that will keep you on the right track? If you are still in a place of hell (professionally or personally), write down your best advice for working your way through this challenging time and coming out the other side.

Kudos, Kiddo(s)!

You have almost made it to the end. You have already learned a bazillion new techniques and done a lot of great work. Let just being nominated be its own reward!

But you do want to win, don't you? Then channel your own inner Meryl Streep, and if you have to learn Polish and German in the next week, then do it. Achtung, baby! Seriously, you have come up with a plan for how to get the gold. Just making that plan is a huge accomplishment.

You looked back on your own life, which is undoubtedly complex and full of some comedy and some errors. You revisited painful times, hard times, and tried to pull some lessons from them that you can use now. And you will use them, baby!

19

the end is the beginning

Today is your final deadline. You did it! You reached your goal, or at least made a huge dent in it. And now you know that you can commit to a project, commit to your writing, and begin the process of channeling the story that was in your head, into the story on the page.

But before we get back to work, on the next section of stories, next drafts, next projects, let's take a moment to acknowledge what's been accomplished and how you accomplished it.

Cue music, please …

And Now the End Is Near …

The key to staying organized is staying organized. So use the logical part of your brain to make notes now (before the ditzy chick or dude in you returns)!

Exercise: My Way

If you did reach your goal, as I hope you did, for corn's sake, take a moment to feel good about it. In this superficial and overstimulating world, it is not easy to accomplish anything. So remember how this feels. If you did not meet your goal, at least acknowledge the progress you made.

So that, like labor pains, this birthing experience is not forgotten …

1. Summarize what your goal was when you first began and what you actually accomplished in the end.

2. Note your methods. What worked well for you; what did not work so well? What did you learn that you can apply to the next project or draft?

Don't overthink this next exercise. Treat it like a job.

Exercise: Next Deadline, Game Plan

1. Write down your next concrete goal (quantify as appropriate with length, page count, etc.) and your deadline for meeting that goal, and mark it down on your calendar.

2. Write out a game plan for yourself for meeting said goal.

Now how about some fun?!

Exercise: Create Your Own Exercises

Come up with 10 exercises to take with you on the next leg of your journey.

Here are three to get you going ...

1. **Draw your character.**

   Take a few minutes to draw a character from your piece. Now on a separate sheet of paper write down everything you notice about your character, based *only* on your drawing.

2. **Write your story as a song.**

   Props to Janet Rosen for this one! Take five minutes to compose your piece as if it were a song.

3. **Concentrate on an object.**

   Concentrate on an object for five minutes, stare at it, embody it, and then describe it, using your five senses. Later, find a way to integrate this description (or use this technique) for your actual project.

You didn't forget about the mission statement from the introduction did you? Well, I didn't. Read on, and complete as directed.

Exercise: Mission Statement

The key, like in most hero's journey–type narratives, is motivation. What is your motivation? What is your heart's desire? Be specific. Personally, fame and fortune were never my major goals. Freedom was. The freedom to write what I wanted and to work with other writers as I wanted, to pay homage to the gods of writing, as I told you in my mission statement, in this book's introduction.

Now try writing your mission statement. One paragraph: the whole truth, pared down.

Write it. Live it.

And now that we've reached the end, let me share some final nuggets.

Just Start

Nothing will ever make you feel better about your writing than writing itself. Yes, you will have bad days, but even on those days if you can pick up a pen, or open your computer, and just jot down an idea, or compose a sentence, you will be on your way.

Structure

Set up who your people are, build to an exciting climax, and then make sure that climax is active; give your readers or viewers a denouement (in other words, bring them down a little before you reach "the end").

Taking Notes

My painter client, Loretta Feeney, who is working on a book about her craft, said that when ideas spring into her head, whether ideas for painting or for writing, "When these things come to you, you better write them down or they are gone."

Character

Form a relationship with your characters, and commit to getting to know these "experimental selves" (as Milan Kundera called them).

When you think you're done, don't stop.

My former client, fellow curator, and dear friend John McCaffrey told me that the best advice I ever gave him was, "When you think you're done, don't stop. Do another hundred words." He said some of his best work has happened "after he was done."

Hate

The best advice I ever got from John was when he came to my old apartment near Times Square on a very terrible February day. A pigeon that had been terrorizing my terrace for years laid eggs right outside my window. Before the eggs cracked, I nearly cracked up (and not with laughter). The maintenance guys dealt with the fowl, but John told me, "Jill, you're a good person, and it's okay for you to hate that pigeon. I mean really let yourself hate it." And I did. I wrote a piece about it that got picked up in a small lit mag. The lesson here? When you are overcome with emotion, especially uncomfortable emotions, feel them, in the extreme. Get visceral, not cerebral.

Sanity

My friend Stanley Richardson said, "Ultimately, it *is* always a (writing) structure that helps me maintain my sanity. The workshop really taught me the importance of making time. I was able to do it, but didn't realize how critical it was to getting things done and feeling in control (of something. If not the quality—or even the quantity—at least the question of whether I'm doing all that I can to write this play)."

Practice. Learn. Practice. Learn.

Give over to the joy of practicing a craft, learning from your mistakes, and getting better.

Learn to end.

If you look at the end of one project as the beautiful pause before the beginning of the next one (like the pause between songs on an album), you will find a way to finish one piece of work, and then begin another, and another ....

One Final Exercise

If you are working with a group, write down a secret wish for another writer in your group.

If you are working solo, write down a secret wish for another writer in your life.

Bang a final key and blow out the candle.

a resource guide for resourceful key-bangers

Chapter 1

Bliven Jr., Bruce. *The Wonderful Writing Machine*. New York: Random House, 1954.

The lecture on the Hebrew letters was given at the Meaningful Life Center by Rabbi Simon Jacobson. See www.meaningfullife.com for more information.

Portions of this chapter were originally published in *The Writer* magazine, November 2007.

Chapter 2

Murray, Donald M. *Writing to Deadline: The Journalist at Work*. Portsmouth, NH: Heinemann, 2000.

Calvino, Italo. *Six Memos for the Next Millennium*. Cambridge, MA: Harvard University Press, 1988.

O'Connor, Flannery. *The Habit of Being.* New York: Farrar Strauss, Giroux, 1979.

Mayers Salkaln, Elaine. "The Mystery Woman," (profile of Leonora Carrington) in *The New York Times*, October 13, 2002.

Chapter 3

Wilde, Oscar. *The Importance of Being Earnest* (play), originally produced 1895.

Capron, Marion. *The Art of Fiction #13*, interview with Dorothy Parker, *The Paris Review*, 195. Posted on www.parisreview.org.

Oates, Joyce Carol. *The Journal of Joyce Carol Oates 1973–1982* New York: Ecco, 2007

Highsmith, Patricia. *Plotting and Writing Suspense Fiction.* New York: St. Martin's Press, 1983.

Wilson, Andrew. *Beautiful Shadow: A Life of Patricia Highsmith.* New York: Bloomsbury, 2003.

Lentine, Genine. "Remembering Stanley Kunitz." www. Poetryfoundation.org. 2007

Naipaul, V. S. "Prologue to an Autobiography" from *Finding the Center: Two Narratives.* New York: Alfred A. Knopf, 1984.

Kafka, Franz. *Diaries,* edited by Max Brod. New York: Schocken Books, 2000.

Auster, Paul. *Hand to Mouth: A Chronicle of Early Failure.* New York: Henry Holt and Company, Inc., 1997.

Chandler, Raymond. *The Notebooks of Raymond Chandler.* Toronto: Penguin Books Canada, 1976.

Hemingway, Ernest. "A Good Café on the Place St.-Michel," from *A Moveable Feast*. New York: Scribner, 1964.

Strindberg, August. *Letters of August Strindberg to Harriet Bose: Love Letters from a Tormented Genius*, edited and translated by Arvid Paulson. New York: Thomas Nelson and Sons, 1959.

Cheever, John. *The Journals of John Cheever* by John Cheever. New York: Ballantine, 1993.

Gluck, Louise. *Proofs and Theories: Essays on Poetry*. New York: Ecco, 1995.

Chapter 5

Lee, Hermione. *Edith Wharton: A Biography*. New York: Vintage Books, 200

Woolf, Virginia, and Leonard Woolf. *A Writer's Diary: Being Extracts from the Diary of Virginia Woolf*. New York: Harcourt Trade, 2003.

Wilde, Oscar. *Lady Windermere's Fan* (play), first produced 1892.

Tomkins, Calvin. "Lifting the Veil" (Profile of John Currin). *The New Yorker*, January 2008.

Chapter 6

Emerson, Ralph Waldo. *The Portable Emerson*. New York: Viking, 1946.

Siegel, Lee. *Against the Machine: Being Human in the Age of the Electronic Mob*. New York: Spiegel and Grau, 2008.

Assadi, Abdi. *Shadows on the Path*. New York: Publicide, 2007.

Rosenberg, Larry, with David Guy. *Breath by Breath: The Liberating Practice of Insight Meditation*. Boston: Shambala, 1998.

Salzberg, Sharon, and Joseph Goldstein. *Insight Meditation*. Boulder, CO: Sounds True, 2001.

Suzuki, Shunryu. *Zen Mind, Beginner's Mind*. Boston: Shambala Library, 2008.

Bloom, Harold, editor. *J.D. Salinger Modern Critical Views*. New York: Chelsea House Publishers, 1987.

Gooding, Mel, editor, and Alastair Brotchie, compiler. *A Book of Surrealist Games*. Boston: Shambala, 1995.

Chapter 7

Bradbury, Ray. *Fahrenheit 451*. London: Harper, 2004.

Chapter 8

Aristotle. *The Poetics of Aristotle*, translated by Preston H. Epps. Chapel Hill, NC: The University of North Carolina Press, 1982.

Chapter 10

Sams, Jamie, and David Carson. *Medicine Cards*. Santa Fe, NM: Bear and Company, 1988.

Chapter 11

Yates, Richard. *Revolutionary Road*. Boston: Little, Brown & Co., 1961.

Bailey, Blake. *A Tragic Honesty: The Life and Work of Richard Yates*. New York: Picador, 2003.

Gladwell, Malcolm. "Late Bloomers." *The New Yorker*, October 2008.

Chapter 12

Jacobi, Jolande, *Complex, Archetype, Symbol in the Psychology of C. G. Jung*, translated by Ralph Manheim. New York: Princeton University Press, 1959.

Cayce, Edgar. *The Edgar Cayce Collection*, edited by Hugh Lynn Cayce. New York: Bonanza Books, 1968.

Epel, Naomi. *Writers Dreaming*. New York: Vintage, 1994.

Lee, Gwen, and Doris Elaine Sauter, editors. *What if Our World Is Their Heaven? The Final Conversations of Philip K. Dick*. Woodstock, NY: Overlook, 2000.

Chapter 13

Rudhyar, Dane. *The Astrological Houses: The Spectrum of Individual Experience*. New York: Doubleday, 1972.

Kundera, Milan. *The Art of the Novel*, translated by Linda Asher. New York: Perennial Library, 1988.

Hirschberg, Lynn. "The Redeemer" (Profile of Pedro Almodovar). *The New York Times Magazine*, September 2004.

Chapter 14

McWilliams, Nancy. *Psychoanalytic Diagnosis: Understanding Personality Structure in the Clinical Process*. New York: The Guildford Press, 1994.

Chapter 16

King, Billie Jean. *Billie Jean King's Secrets of Winning Tennis.* New York: Holt, Rinehart and Winston, 1974.

Queneau, Raymond. *Exercises in Style.* New York: New Directions, 1947.

Grimm, Jacob, and Wilhelm Grimm. *Grimm's Fairy Tales,* consulting editorial director George Stade. New York: Barnes and Noble Classics, 2003.

Hamilton, Edith. *Mythology: Timeless Tales of Gods and Heroes.* New York: Penguin, 1969.

Chapter 17

Siegel, Lee. "Eyes Wide Shut: What the Critics Failed to See in Kubrick's Last Film." *Harper's Magazine,* October 1999.

Dalai Lama, H. H., with Howard C. Cutler. *The Essence of Happiness.* London: Hodder Headline, 2002.

Additional Reading and Resources for Jill Dearman's *Bang the Keys* Immersion Course ...

The resources that follow were mentioned in the book *and* will fill out your writer's library nicely.

Books

Alexander, Paul. *Salinger: A Biography.* Los Angeles: Renaissance Books, 1999.

Barthes, Roland. *Mythologies.* London: J. Cape, 1972.

Bazin, Andre. *What is Cinema?,* edited and translated by Hugh Gray. Berkeley: University of California Press, 2004.

Bell, Susan. *The Artful Edit*. New York: WW Norton and Company, 2007.

Bloom, Harold. *Kabbalah and Criticism*. London: Continuum, 2005.

Borges, Jorge Luis. *This Craft of Verse*, edited by Calin-Andrei Mihailescu. Cambridge, MA: Harvard University Press, 2000.

Bradbury, Ray *Zen in the Art of Writing*. Santa Barbara, CA: Joshua Odell Editions, 1990.

Egri, Lajos. *The Art of Dramatic Writing*. New York: Simon and Schuster, 1960.

Gornick, Vivian. *The Situation and the Story*. New York: Farrar, Straus, and Giroux, 2002.

Irving, John. *My Movie Business*. New York: Ballantine, 2000.

Moffett, James, and Kenneth R. McElheny, editors. *Points of View*. New York: Mentor, 1995.

Prose, Francine. *Reading Like a Writer*. New York: Harper Collins, 2006

Truss, Lynne. *Eats, Shoots & Leaves*. New York: Gotham Books, 2004.

Websites for Writers

If you have to avoid your work a tiny bit by surfing online, please bookmark the sites of these invaluable writers' resources!

www.awpwriters.org

www.brooklynwriters.com

www.cantaraville.com

www.pw.org

www.writermag.com

www.riversedgewriters.com

www.writersdigest.com

www.writersmarket.com

www.writersrelief.com

www.writersroom.org

Custom-Made Writing Cahiers

www.bangthekeys.com

Support for Writers

www.robertmcveytherapy.com

Work of Clients and Friends Mentioned in the Text

www.facebook.com/profile.php?id=791246257 (Brooke Berman)

www.misscecil.com (Cecil Castellucci)

www.mayaciarrocchi.com (Maya Ciarrocchi)

www.widesphere.com (Wendy Jo Cohen)

www.imdb.com (Chris Downey)

www.imdb.com (Scott Duffy)

www.lorettafeeney.com (Loretta Feeney)

www.bangthekeys.com (Hope Forstenzer)

www.robingaines.com (Robin Gaines)

web.mac.com/pgianopoulos (Panio Gianopoulos)

www.bangthekeys.com (Starr Goode)

www.dalethcareyhall.blogspot.com (Daleth Carey Hall)

www.shotmonster.com (Matthew Howe).

www.andreakleine.com (Andrea Kleine)

www.cmlperformance.org (Paintings by Iris Lezak)

www.cmlperformance.org (Clarinda Mac Low)

www.jamccaffrey.com (John McCaffrey)

www.joemoran.info (Joe Moran)

www.jenniferneal.net (Jennifer Neal)

www.101crustaceans.com (Ed Pastorini)

Nothing But You: Love Stories of The New Yorker (includes "Sculpture 1" by Angela Patrinos).

www.imdb.com/name/nm1301702 (Judith Pinsker)

www.bangthekeys.com (Stan Richardson)

The Fairy Flag and Other Stories (Jim Savio)

www.bangthekeys.com (Jeremy Seaver)

www.bangthekeys.com (Seema Srivastava)

www.charlesbstrozier.com (Charles B. Strozier)

Magazine Editors Talk to Writers by Judy Mandell (includes interview with Claudia Valentino)

www.compassrosemagazine.blogspot.com/2008/03/
r-elena-pearson-and-laura-esther.html (Laura Esther Wolfson)

www.fictionweekly.com/TheEvolutionOfTulips.htm
(Lauren Yaffe)

Anything and everything else: www.jilldearman.com

index